Second-Chance DOGS

True Stories *of the* Dogs We Rescue
and the Dogs Who Rescue Us

Callie Smith Grant, ed.

Revell
a division of Baker Publishing Group
Grand Rapids, Michigan

© 2018 by Callie Smith Grant

Published by Revell
a division of Baker Publishing Group
PO Box 6287, Grand Rapids, MI 49516-6287
www.revellbooks.com

Printed in the United States of America

Library of Congress Cataloging-in-Publication Data
Names: Grant, Callie Smith, author.
Title: Second-chance dogs : true stories of the dogs we rescue and the dogs who rescue us / Callie Smith Grant.
Description: Grand Rapids : Revell-Baker Publishing Group, 2018. | Includes bibliographical references and index.
Identifiers: LCCN 2018010008 | ISBN 9780800727130 (pbk. : alk. paper)
Subjects: LCSH: Dog owners—Religious life. | Rescue dogs—Anecdotes. | Dogs—Religious aspects—Christianity—Anecdotes.
Classification: LCC BV4596.A54 G73 2018 | DDC 636.7/08320929—dc23
LC record available at https://lccn.loc.gov/2018010008

20   21   22   23   24   7   6   5   4

In keeping with biblical principles of creation stewardship, Baker Publishing Group advocates the responsible use of our natural resources. As a member of the Green Press Initiative, our company uses recycled paper when possible. The text paper of this book is composed in part of post-consumer waste.

Second-Chance
DOGS

Other Books by Callie Smith Grant

To rescue organizations everywhere,
the exceptional people who keep them going,
and the kind, smart individuals who take abandoned animals
into their homes and their hearts.

Contents

Introduction

Callie Smith Grant

Rescue. It's a good word, isn't it? Who would have thought the day would come when it could be trendy to say about your dog, "He's a rescue." Or "She was found wandering on Main Street . . ." We've always known a dog doesn't need a pedigree to be a wonder. He or she simply needs a chance—often a second chance.

In *Second-Chance Dogs: True Stories of the Dogs We Rescue and the Dogs Who Rescue Us*, you'll meet dogs either getting a most-needed second chance or giving that second chance to someone else. These dogs come from shelters and pounds, breeders and breed rescue groups, homegrown litters and the streets. Their stories take place across the United States plus Canada, Panama, St. Martin, Germany, France, and Greece—showing how universal and unique rescues can be.

Many of these stories demonstrate how dogs have ways of paying forward any grace extended to them. It's as if they say, "Let me move in, and I promise you'll be glad." Then they somehow do things like save lives for the people who chose them or the animals around them or even strangers who cross their paths. Or they provide much-needed comfort or companionship to the lonely or frightened. Sometimes it's a big bombastic achievement. Sometimes it's subtle. My husband and I had moved to a new town and were looking for a church. We found one whose members care about each other and the community, and we eventually joined.

But I will confess that what sealed the deal for me was that this church allows dogs. Yes, this handsome, historic church that had been downtown for over 150 years welcomes dogs. We don't happen to have a dog, and few dogs attend. But they are welcome. And I like that.

One young woman used to bring her aging Chihuahua to church. This very mellow dog would take any attention in stride, rolling her round, pretty eyes at people. I always felt privileged when I could have the dog sitting in my pew.

We had a parishioner who suffered a stroke. She came back to church, but she could no longer talk or even smile—and she had been outgoing. When the part of the service came where we all shake hands and hug each other in the aisle, I could see why she seemed so melancholy—people spoke to her and smiled at her, but she simply could not reciprocate in the same way. The stroke had taken that ability.

One Sunday, the Chihuahua and her human sat next to the lady who'd had the stroke. During the service, the woman surprised me by reaching out for the little dog, and the dog was handed to her. Then something unexpected happened. The woman began to verbalize to the dog—loudly, garbled, and with expression. Nobody could understand a word, but clearly she was emoting to the quiet little dog in her arms. It was as if she was releasing all her pent-up personal pain and her lack of ability to communicate to this creature who looked into her eyes and seemed to understand every word.

The entire congregation grew silent, and a few quietly wept. We knew we were watching something extraordinary, because what none of us could do with a hug, a handshake, or a smile, the dog did.

I've always believed this kind of animal is God-sent. The Chihuahua was not the older woman's dog, but to me, they crossed paths for a healing purpose. The connection between human and animal for that moment was strong and obvious, and the Chihuahua helped the woman once again feel understood—and once again feel at home.

Home. That's another beautiful word. It is telling how many of these stories have that word in their titles. So a dog gets a home. A home gets a dog. A home is complete, thanks to the marvelous beasts in *Second-Chance Dogs*.

Bringing Honey Home

Andrea Doering

The day we visited the rescue shelter, it's fair to say there were at least four desired outcomes in our family of five. There was my husband's version, which was predicated on the idea that because he'd stayed at home, no real decision could be made about a dog, and confirmed the premise we were "just looking."

There was our daughter Emily's version, which entailed us breezing through the adult dog section, onward to the puppy room, and at the sight of all that cuddly fluff, Emily's mother's reservations about a puppy would melt.

There was my version, which assumed that just before we arrived at the shelter, someone would drop off a perfectly trained King Charles spaniel that loved children and was very quiet.

Henry and Katherine, our twins, shared their desired outcome. Generally, Henry's plans were what Katherine deemed best for him; it made life easier, and he could get on with the important stuff, like Legos or Pokémon cards. And on this day, Katherine's desired outcome was a dog to love. The winter was over, a brisk, clear spring Saturday was ahead of us, and already Katherine had visions of walking her dog, playing with her dog at the park or on the beach, and sneaking her dog into her bed. Henry's only demand in this shared plan was a big dog, one with heft.

We piled out of the car and into the shelter, each of us with our vision of how we would exit—Emily with her puppy, me with a King Charles spaniel, the twins with a dog, largeish in size. Spirits were high as we walked through and looked at dogs and their descriptions. We were not good, we realized, at choosing a dog by consensus. The few we chose to spend time with in the common area of the shelter were compromise dogs for all of us, and they seemed to know it. We walked around again. The first time around, Katherine and I had stopped at the cage of a hound who immediately left the far corner and came to take a sniff of this young girl. But no one else was thinking this was our dog, so we moved on.

On our second pass through, Katherine approached the same cage and was distraught to find it empty. One of the volunteers assured her that the dog, Honey, was likely just out on a walk. Being new to the dog rescue world, we really didn't know how long that walk would take, and by now the morning was gone and lunch seemed like a good idea.

On the promise that we would return another day, we made our exit. With so many possible outcomes, somehow we had managed the least likely one—the one championed by the guy not even in the car. As we pulled out of the parking lot, I saw Katherine glance back at the building, at the dogs going on their walks, at people coming and going with dogs. She turned her head away from me, but the disappointment was so thick it was almost visible in the space between us.

I miss a lot as a mom. I know I've missed my children's hurt feelings and glad tidings and dashed hopes. And on this day I can't say I was being particularly intentional. I was likely thinking about what I had at the house to make for lunch. But I will ever be grateful that I didn't miss that look on my young daughter's face.

I slowed the car and moved into the turn lane, saying, "Katherine, we should go back, don't you think? Maybe that hound is back from her walk now."

That hound, Honey, was back, and greeted Katherine with a leap up as if they'd been separated too long already. And though Honey was always, from that day, more Katherine's dog than anyone else's, Katherine's vision of what having a dog would mean had to shift. Honey came home with us, shy and quiet. For weeks she didn't want to stray far from the house. For four years, she didn't reciprocate cuddles. And during the time we were graced with her life, she never fetched things that were thrown, and she wouldn't sleep on anyone's bed. She was a Treeing Walker Coonhound, and what she loved to do was catch a scent and follow it. But though Wikipedia says this breed is known for their "distinctive bay," Honey never barked. Ever.

Katherine had another vision for Honey she didn't share with us at the time but has since told me. She envisioned a leash-less world for her (and every other dog), where Honey could run and run, full tilt with ears flapping and mouth in that wide open smile, catching every scent possible. And when she'd had enough, she would lope back home and sit on the front step, waiting for someone to let her inside to her soft bed and clean water. It turned out Honey was completely on board for that vision! Before we wised up to the need for a harness, she was a master at weaseling out of her collar and taking off at a gallop. After a few escapes, this we did find out—Honey knew her way back home.

We all became smitten with our quiet hound, who loved sun and scent but hardly bothered to lift her head when we came in the door. Though she let the kids lie on her belly, dress her up, or move her around, she was kind of the anti-family dog, allowing affection but reluctant to give her own. Somehow, though, her quiet patience resonated with all sorts of people. The daycare workers in town made it a point to walk their kids down our street so they could say hello to Honey as she basked in the afternoon sun in the yard. The postman, instead of giving us the "please keep your dog inside" notice, offered her treats. In appreciation, Honey memorized the striped pattern of both postal worker uniforms and their vehicles, and would stop anywhere she saw one, waiting for a morsel.

During all these years, a lot more was taking place in our little quintet—the three children were in the throes of middle school, the parents were navigating job losses and job changes, an uncertain economy, and the failing health of their own parents. There were times none of us wanted to talk to each other. But we all participated in caring for Honey—walking, bathing, feeding, rubbing that pink spotted belly in the sunshine. Even my husband, the one who originally thought "no dog" was an option (Oh, Ron!), made sure she got what she needed and much of what she wanted. On tough days, when I couldn't find any kind words to share with anyone, I'd put a leash on her and take a walk, talk to her, and things would be all right.

Some days the only being any of us liked in the house was this quiet hound. Some of the best memories I have of those years involve everyone home watching a movie on a Saturday night, Honey right in front of the television with Henry sprawled out on one side and Katherine curled up on the other. Day by day, she knit our family together. It's not far-fetched to say she saved us from unraveling during those years.

The fifth year Honey lived with us, one thing started to change— she seemed as happy to be with us as we were with her. She began getting up to greet us at the door, and come sit by us in the evening, pushing her side against our knees, turning to get another ear scratched. She would thump her tail when the kids came to find her after school, sniffing for news of their day.

I am not one who understands the way of dogs, so I have no idea what that meant from her point of view. But I know what it

18

meant for us, the humans in her life. What she'd started five years earlier by capturing Katherine's heart blossomed into a great calm that came over an anxious family. That year, when Honey began to respond to our consistent ministrations on her behalf, it seemed as though she liked us. If this hound could like us, and trust us, well . . . maybe we could trust ourselves and our capabilities. I don't know of a greater gift anyone can offer to another.

Bruce

Donna Acton

When I teach my six-week dog obedience class, I spend part of one session on guard dog training. On television, you see a lot of snarling and barking and police officers sending their dogs to chase, bite, and bring down the bad guy. I explain to my students that as the responsible owners of a family dog, they will spend 99.9 percent of their time calling their dog off their aggression toward people. In most instances, the people at our front doors or in our yards are meter readers, postal carriers, UPS and FedEx drivers, or Girl Scouts selling cookies. We want all these people to be able to approach our homes without being in danger from our dogs.

My personal experience has been that once or twice in the lifetime of each dog I have owned, I've needed that dog to step up to the plate and protect me. Or at least act like they will. Acting is a very important concept here. Bruce taught me that when I was a teenager.

As the daughter of a veterinarian who had built his home and clinic with a connecting door between them, I basically grew up in a veterinary hospital. Our personal pets were often abandoned animals brought in by Good Samaritans and in need of medical help.

The four-month-old Weimaraner puppy came to us a little differently. His owner brought him in with broken front legs and a broken jaw after the dog was hit by a truck. After my father showed the man the X-rays and discussed the long-term healing process, the owner asked if the puppy would be able to hunt when he grew up. My father said that due to the severity of the injuries, the odds were not good for him to have the kind of physical stamina he would need for hunting.

The owner shook his head. "I'm not going to invest money in a dog that can't hunt. I'll just cut my losses and have him put down."

Dad said, "Do you mind if I fix him up the best I can and keep him for my kids?"

"As long as I don't have to pay for it," the owner replied.

So we had a new family dog, and we named him Bruce. His front legs never caught up in growth with his back legs, so he always looked like he was walking downhill. But he was a great pet who would live to be fourteen.

I was the only person who spent any time training Bruce or teaching him commands. Nobody else in my family was interested in learning how or thought it was necessary. They would just let him out the front door when he was barking at a person ringing the doorbell, then yell at the person, "He won't hurt you." Bruce would run straight past the stranger, who invariably looked horrified, and bound into the front yard about twenty feet, come to a dead stop, and bark senselessly up into a big oak tree. After a few minutes, he would wander around to the back door of our house, ask to be let in, and then politely invite the new person to pet him. I think Bruce enjoyed going through the motions of acting like a guard dog. But Bruce was a hunting dog by nature, so his heart wasn't really into intimidating people.

When I was in high school, I went through a phase where I could never find my shoes in the morning before the bus came—and missing the bus meant big trouble in our house. One morning

I was standing at the front door, fully dressed and holding my books, but with no shoes. In total desperation, I finally looked into Bruce's eyes and said, "Go fetch my shoes!"

Bruce trotted across the living room and down the hallway to the back bedrooms. I waited. I did wonder what was going to happen, because this was the first time I had ever uttered the words "go fetch" to him. Then Bruce appeared with one of my shoes. I was elated. I was relieved. I said, "Go fetch!" again.

The dog left me at a dead run and reappeared with my other shoe. He did this every morning for an entire year of high school. I never taught him to retrieve my shoes, and he never brought me anything else or anybody else's shoes, even though there were five other people in the house. To this day, I don't know how or where he found them when I could not. At the time I was just thankful to get to the bus stop on time. And that Bruce and I were on the same wavelength.

One Sunday I was home alone, which was odd in itself. Usually there were weekend employees or my family around. But not this day.

The ringing doorbell sent Bruce to the front door. He weighed a bit over a hundred pounds, and he had a deep, throaty bark. Because of his broken jaw, his lower canine teeth were always exposed, which made him appear to be snarling. It was very intimidating.

Our house/hospital was just off the exit ramp of the highway, so we were used to stranded motorists walking to the door and asking to use our phone in these pre-cell phone days. People also came to the front door of the house after hours with animal medical emergencies. I was expecting either of those two scenarios when I heard the front doorbell, but this day turned out to be different.

Over Bruce's barking through the unlocked screen door, a man asked if he could use our phone. He was a young guy, in his twenties with long, stringy hair. At first I thought hippie, Woodstock, peace and love. Then I looked into his eyes and thought, not hippie, more like Charles Manson. In fact, the hair on the back of my neck stood up.

I had trained Bruce, as I had all of our family dogs, not to approach or bother any of our patients or their owners in the clinic or parking lot. But the front door and doorbell of the house were fair game. Someone knocking or ringing was Bruce's cue to bark. His protective and alerting behavior was acceptable until my call-off signal.

Now I looked at Bruce, who was still barking. He looked back at me questioningly. I could tell Bruce was waiting for me to call him off like I had done a hundred times before and was wondering what the holdup was. To call Bruce off when he was barking, I always used a voice command and a hand signal. I never grabbed his collar. Touching him empowered him, as it does all dogs, and would make him start lunging and dragging me forward.

When I quickly decided not to let this stranger inside, I looked at Bruce and thought, *Keep barking.* Bruce looked back at me as if to say, *Really? Keep barking?*

Yes! I looked back at him and grabbed onto his collar, knowing it would amplify his display. The moment I touched his collar, my fear and anxiety shot down my arm and into his body. He could feel the hair standing up on the back of my neck. His eyes went from questioning to the shock of understanding and knowing: *Danger!*

If he had appeared threatening before, he now looked truly horrifying. Barking faster, snarling louder, Bruce was now flashing his teeth in the man's face with each bark. Like a choreographed dance, Bruce lunged and dragged me forward to the thin screen of the door, barking like he was crazy.

I looked the man straight in the eye and lied. "I can't let you in. The dog bites."

The stringy-haired man looked at Bruce. Then he looked back at me. I held my breath. What if he asked me to make a call for him? What if he put his hand on the handle of the unlocked screen door? What if he pulled the door open? There were only two feet between us, a mere twenty-four inches.

But he said, "That's okay. Thanks anyway."

And just like that, he turned on his heel and walked away.

I let go of Bruce, slammed the big wooden front door shut, and locked it. A great wave of relief washed over me.

But Bruce didn't feel any relief. No call-off signal, my fear—these were all new to him. His blood was up, and he felt the need for action. Barking, he raced to the kitchen door, then to the sliding glass door in the dining room. I ran to the living room and looked out the bay window. The long-haired man was crossing our parking lot, heading back to the highway entrance ramp at a quick clip and not looking back.

I didn't need a dog that day to chase, bite, or bring down the bad guy. I just needed a family dog, like Bruce, trained to let everybody come and go, day in and day out—but who would act like he would attack and bite when I decided circumstances called for it.

The other important thing I learned from Bruce was how much a dog can feel our fear without a word being spoken.

I experienced this again a few years later when I was driving from Michigan to Arkansas. Looking at the map, I decided that St. Louis, Missouri, would be a good place to spend the night at a motel. As I neared St. Louis, I spotted a sign that said "Holiday Inn, Next Exit." I put on my blinker. Bruce, who had been sleeping in the back seat since Ft. Wayne, raised his head when he felt me apply the brakes.

What a surprise I had at the stop sign at the end of the exit ramp. There was no Holiday Inn or signage to point the way. There were no stores, no houses, and no businesses. As far as the eye could see was pavement crisscrossed by railroad tracks, weed-choked parking lots, and huge industrial buildings in the distance. No traffic and no people. All around me was a forest of cement piers rising fifty to a hundred feet in the air, balancing the numerous highways arcing across the sky.

I looked in the rearview mirror just as a beater car with no muffler and five scruffy men pulled up behind me, revving their engine. My heart was in my throat. The hair stood up on the back of my neck. I immediately realized I shouldn't be here. I also realized, as I sat stupefied at the stop sign, that I had no idea how to get back to the highway.

That is when Bruce went into action. He stood up, wild-eyed, and started barking insanely. He raced back and forth between the rear windows barking, barking, barking. He leapt from the back seat to the front seat to the back seat to the front, barking, barking, barking.

All I could think was not only am I in a very bad place but now the dog has gone crazy. Taking another look in the rearview mirror, I saw the faces of the five men. They were watching Bruce also. They looked pretty shocked.

I hit the gas. I didn't care if I was on a street or not. I rumbled across railroad tracks, bounced through potholes, and steered around cement curbs. Bruce continued barking and jumping from the front to the back seat. Then I saw a sign with an arrow that said "To Tulsa." With a huge sigh of relief, I made my way back up, onto the divided highway strung like gray cement ribbons above the city of St. Louis. The moment I reached seventy-five miles per hour, without a word from me, Bruce stopped barking. He could feel that the tension was gone. He lay down and fell asleep instantly.

That night Bruce and I stayed at a mom-and-pop motel on the side of the highway thirty minutes west of St. Louis. It looked like Norman Bates owned it. I told the lady at the front desk I had a dog, but didn't mention how big he was.

The lady thoughtfully eyed me and asked, "Is he a good dog?"

"Yes, he is," I said.

She handed me the room key.

I showered that night with Bruce locked in the bathroom with me. He slept on the other double bed in the room, nearest the door. I never felt safer.

People often tell me they want a good watch dog. What I learned from Bruce was that the minute the hair stands up on the back of your neck and fear engulfs you, you don't have to say anything. Your dog will know. He can feel what you feel.

So I tell those people not to worry. If they are truly afraid, their dog will know it immediately and come to their aid. Bruce always did.

The dog who was almost put down because he was of no use for hunting was a godsend to me.

Dust Bunnies

Susy Flory

Sprinkles was more of a Facebook dog than a rescue dog. While I'd like to say that I went to an animal shelter and asked them for the dog that had been there the longest so I could give it a happy home, the truth is I was browsing around on Facebook one day and saw photos of a passel of silky terrier puppies. They looked like little fluffy brown and cream porcupines with shiny black button eyes.

At that moment I had no particular intention of acquiring a puppy. Even if I had, I would never have picked a terrier. I was used to big mellow dogs.

But something inside me fell in love with those terrier puppies, and love makes us do crazy and even dangerous things. The heart wants what it wants, especially if there's a puppy involved.

My fifteen-year-old daughter and I went to see the puppies, and the one who chose us was a tiny female we named Sprinkles, named after the sprinkles on a cupcake (although I will admit she has distributed some doggie sprinkles on the carpet from time to time). Sprinkles joined our household and, frankly, she was a lot of work. I'd never had an inside dog before, much less the tiny, feisty kind. There was housetraining and barking. Our floors were littered with rope toys and buck-naked tennis balls. And the crowning touch—on her first week in the house, Sprinkles mountain-climbed her tiny self up a double flight of stairs, jumped on our bed, and left an artistically composed pile of poop in the exact middle of my husband's pillow. It would have been funny, except he didn't want an inside dog. Actually, if I'm being completely honest, my daughter and I had tricked him into this whole small-dog-in-the-house thing in the first place.

Ever since I'd casually mentioned I might just want an inside dog to replace my son when he left for college (moms have a hole in their heart when their kids leave, you know), he'd put his shiny leather loafer down.

"No inside dogs." Period. End of story.

Except I'm not an end-of-story kind of person. I'm more of a work-around kind of person, a choose-your-own-ending kind of person, a let-go-and-let-God kind of person. I like to live in dreams and possibilities and what-ifs. I've seen God do some crazy-amazing things, and who am I to live out a boring, prescriptive life? I like a bit of adventure.

So I waited for the right time to let my husband in on this new furry adventure. My daughter and I strategically planned out the moment of Sprinkles's arrival and took some measures to smooth the way for her forced entry into our household. We went to the store and picked up the ingredients for a delicious meal, including a big, juicy steak. We baked cupcakes. We set a beautiful table, then my daughter went upstairs to wait with Sprinkles for the right moment. It was sort of like Esther waiting and praying for the right moment to approach the king of Persia with her request for help. We needed help, and her name was Sprinkles.

My husband ate his steak dinner and seemed relaxed and happy. I texted my daughter, and she came downstairs with the cutest puppy ever. My husband was surprised, but who could resist, especially on a full tummy?

Overall it went well, although later I did receive a few "Your dog did this!" photos and texts when it turned out she was just a tiny bit difficult to housetrain.

Over time, Sprinkles learned where to pee and my husband learned to coexist, and things grew more peaceful as she integrated into our household. There was something about stroking her back that was soothing. She greeted everyone at the front door with excitement and a smile. She made us all laugh when her terrier genes emerged and she'd shake her toy to kill it, or busily dig a hole in the side yard, front paws going ninety miles an hour. When we went on walks, her joy was infectious.

Sometimes there was a little too much joy, the terrier kind of joy, if you know what I mean. When she was excited, her whole body showed it—tail straight up like a little flag as she bounced around or streaked around the house like she was on turbo. She could quickly go into a rocket-fueled zone of excitement where it was hard to get her attention. It was doggie ADHD, where she was ready for whatever life might throw at her and her energy level was off the charts.

But one day, when I let her out the side door and then followed her down the steps into the backyard, she wasn't her usual excitable self. Sprinkles was a few steps ahead of me, and I expected her to follow the usual routine—running around the backyard with nose to the ground, checking her pee-mail and seeing what other creatures had left her a message.

This time was different. She was in the middle of some shrubbery and standing stone-still like a little doggie statue, every muscle locked into place. Her head was down, back straight, and tail up.

Then I noticed something strange. Her right front foot was elevated, bent at the knee and hanging in space. At first I couldn't figure out what she was doing. I called her a few times.

"Sprinkles . . . come here."

No response.

"Sprinkles, what are you doing? Come on, come here!"

Nothing.

Then an image popped into my head. I remembered a framed picture on a neighbor's wall of a dog pointing at a pheasant off in the distance. The dog's head was lowered, tail up, and front foot raised. The dog was pointing at the bird with his nose to show the hunter where the bird was. I recognized the posture, now on live display right in front of me. Sprinkles was no bird dog, but she was pointing her nose at something. But what?

I approached with caution. We lived on the edge of a small riparian woodland with a creek. It could have been anything—raccoon, possum, snake—or something worse. *Ugh. What am I going to find?*

As I tiptoed my way into the shrubs, Sprinkles held her ground. She was poised, like a ballet dancer en pointe. She looked like she was holding her breath.

I looked down where she was pointing and didn't see much. *Whew. What a relief.* Just some fluffy debris that looked like dust bunnies.

"Come on, Sprinkles," I said. "Let's go inside."

But she refused to leave. She was still frozen, still pointing.

I looked closer and then my eyes focused on what she was looking at. The dust bunnies were really two tiny baby birds, covered in grayish brown fluff and lying on the ground.

I grabbed Sprinkles around the middle and picked her up, as I tried to figure out what to do. They looked bad. Dead or dying bad. One had worms on it.

It seemed too late, and I felt it was perhaps best to let nature take its course, so I left and went inside. "Good dog, Sprinkles," I said, petting her as we walked up the stairs. I was a little sad, but also happy Sprinkles hadn't tried to hurt them. And I was more than a little proud of her pointing. She had tried to communicate with me, even though it was clearly too late for those two poor little creatures.

Fifteen minutes later my daughter came home from school. She fixed herself a snack as we chatted about her day. Then I remembered. "You'll never guess what Sprinkles did today!"

"What?" she said, half listening as she stirred a bowl of ice cream into liquid.

"Sprinkles found some baby birds that fell out of a nest and she pointed at them."

"Where are they?" she said, her voice full of energy and excitement. I couldn't quite comprehend the question. My point had been how *exciting* it was that Sprinkles had pointed, and that I had noticed. But she didn't seem at all interested in that extraordinary fact. "Show me where they are," she said, throwing her spoon into the bowl with a *clink* and jumping up from the table.

"Okay, I'll show you. But I think they're dead. It looked like they've been out there for a while."

She hustled down the stairs into the backyard with me trailing, and I showed her the spot. The two fluff balls were still there, and looked worse than before. They were limp and lifeless and cold. *This is hopeless.*

But she squatted down, looked at them with what I can only describe as motherly love, and picked them up one at a time with her right hand, placing them carefully onto her left palm. Then she walked slowly up the stairs and into the house, while giving me my orders. "Get a towel, a box, and the heat lamp. And I need some tweezers."

Her voice had changed. She had suddenly transformed into authoritative, powerful, and passionate. I was a little stunned.

Fast forward twelve hours, and I was even more surprised. The two dying baby birds were now sitting up in the box, mouths gaping, and they were very, very much alive. She had picked off the worms with the tweezers, warmed the birds up, Googled what to feed them, and stayed up all night long to feed them every half hour. Sprinkles stayed by her side, watching with interest.

The next morning, I woke up and found my daughter with the resurrected babies. She was exhausted but proud and still radiating love. She was happy. She couldn't quite believe what had happened. Neither could I. Somehow, she had singlehandedly brought two tiny baby birds from death to life.

Later that day, we took the birds to the local wildlife rescue center, where they were identified as California towhees, a plump, medium-sized brown bird common to the San Francisco Bay Area. They often nest in shrubbery.

We watched in wonder as they welcomed the birds into a shiny bustling facility full of busy people with intent looks on their faces. It was an animal ICU, and my daughter instantly fell in love with every single person there. She'd found her tribe.

Five years later, she began working in wildlife rehabilitation in the Sierra Nevada. Now a full-time wildlife "rehabber," she has become an expert and works with all manner of creatures, including owls, hawks, hummingbirds, skunks, squirrels, and deer. She speaks their language, feels their pain, and tries to help however she can, even if it's gently holding an injured creature taking its last breaths. Part of her job is providing hospice care for these wild ones, a heartbreaking job but beautiful in its own way.

Be a righteous dog guardian!

Proverbs 12:10 begins, "The righteous care for the needs of their animals . . ."

All of this (meaning our daughter finding her purpose in life), if you could trace it back like following a silken thread in a complex piece of embroidery, started in our backyard that day when Sprinkles found those two dust bunnies.

Strangely enough, Sprinkles has never again been part of the rescue of an injured animal, nor has she ever pointed again. It was a one-off situation. But in this case, once was enough, because that moment gave my daughter a precious gift—a career and a calling in wildlife rescue. It's a difficult way to make a living with no clear career path, but her passion for it and her knowledge of it grows every day. She's now dreaming about starting a college for people who want to pursue this career.

And if Sprinkles ever points again, you can bet I will pay close attention to what she's found.

The Lieutenant Who Had a Hundred Dogs

Dusty Rainbolt

Dad loved animals, all kinds of animals: dogs, cats, cows, but especially dogs. Until the day he died, he adored them. That love helped him endure the harrowing days of World War II.

Unlike many of the Greatest Generation who kept their war experiences locked deep within their souls, Dad shared some of his stories. Some were amusing, some were horrifying. I remember as a child, sitting on the floor in rapt attention while Dad recalled his missions as a communications scout in France and Germany. I heard his stories countless times, and no matter how often I heard them, they never got old. My one regret was not listening with a reporter's ear and asking for more details, but this is what I remember.

Dad was assigned to the Seventh Army's Signal Corps under General Alexander Patch, and he commanded a small squad of around thirty men. Dad was proud of the fact that all of his men survived the war and returned to their families. Unlike most soldiers who traveled with a large unit, Dad and his men worked free-range, pressing ahead to set up radio and telephone communications. Through my research I've learned that the Seventh Army distinguished itself in formidable winter conditions. Blizzards were the order of the day. I often imagined Dad and his driver, Clifford Linley, maneuvering their unheated jeep through several feet of snow with only personally fashioned spring-loaded doors (that popped off with only a touch during air raids) and a canvas roof to shield them from the cold.

During the course of the war, Dad's men would feed or rescue starving stray dogs they found along the way. But the army frowned on keeping pets. If a pet was discovered, orders could be given to shoot it. However, some officers turned a blind eye to the prohibited pets for the good of both their men and the strays. Lieutenant J. D. Rainbolt was one of those officers. An avid dog lover since childhood, he took no official notice of his soldiers' canine companions. Knowing Dad, however, he most likely offered plenty of unofficial ear scratches and belly rubs.

Dad truly was one of the Greatest Generation. They saved the world, and Dad had his hand in it. He was a champion of the defenseless but in his own subtle, humble way. On one occasion he drove up on some French soldiers who were forcing their young German prisoners to dig their own graves before executing them. Dad stopped them, took the prisoners away, and sent them to the rear, where they were processed as very relieved prisoners of war.

To Dad, *holocaust* was more than a page in a history book. He witnessed man's ultimate inhumanity to man firsthand. Two weeks before the German surrender, Dad was on a mission to set up communications ahead of the advancing American army preparing to capture Munich. Dad and his driver were the first Americans to encounter the horrific concentration camp just outside of Landsberg, Germany. As far as Dad knew, the Americans did not have the slightest inkling of its existence. The barbaric compound turned out to be only one of a network of eleven slave labor prisons discovered near Landsberg.

As their jeep crossed a small bridge, the air grew heavy with the smell of death. Dad described the smoke and stench stinging his nostrils as they approached a barbed wire compound. Nearby boxcars smoldered, failing to erase evidence of atrocities. The Germans had already abandoned the camp and taken the prisoners who had been capable of walking to the main Dachau camp, but hundreds of weak and sick inmates had been left behind. The barbed wire gates had already been forced wide open, and skeletal Jewish women dressed in white and black stripes stood outside the entrance, holding out plates of freshly baked cookies, gifts for their American liberators. How strange that must have been to be offered gifts of food from starving prisoners. Dad never mentioned whether or not he tried the cookies.

Dad had his orders, so he could offer no assistance except to call back and alert the approaching 7th Army about this horrifying discovery. I can't imagine the helplessness of witnessing such brutality and having to move on. I'm sure the scars of that day followed Dad his entire life. He never talked about that. I know his driver, Linley, never discussed the war with his family.

A few weeks later, Dad learned that despite the German surrender, he and his men weren't scheduled to ship home for two more months. In Dad's eyes, that wasn't acceptable. His men needed to be with their families. A man of action, he wandered from ship to ship until he found a transport with room for his squad.

After informing his men they would be shipping out later that day, one of his guys asked, "Lieutenant, what do we do with our dogs?"

Dad told the soldier, "You can't bring them on the ship. Find local families to give them homes. Give them some money so they can afford to feed them."

When the men boarded the troop transport, there wasn't a dog in sight. Dad assumed the locals had a lot of wonderful new pets.

Several hours after weighing anchor, however, dogs started appearing on deck, a few at first and then more and more. Before long, Dad was bumping into pooches no matter where he went on the ship. Dad learned that the soldiers had fed their dogs sedatives, stuffed them in their duffel bags, and then carried them onboard. And Dad's men weren't the only canine smugglers. Most of the dogs onboard had traveled with combat units. Over a hundred French mutts boarded the ship bound for the United States.

The no-nonsense admiral in charge of the convoy ordered my dad to have every dog on the ship shot and thrown overboard.

Dad, never afraid to offer legitimate feedback, replied that killing the dogs was unwise.

The admiral raised his eyebrows condescendingly. "Really? Why?"

"These men are war-hardened," Dad reminded him. "If you start shooting their dogs, there will be a bloodbath. These men won't hesitate to protect their pets."

The admiral wanted to know how these soldiers would carry out such a mutiny since all of the weapons had been stowed below in the bowels of the ship. But only the US military–issued weapons were locked up. The same duffel bags that smuggled contraband dogs also (legally) contained captured guns, ammo, and knives. Before the admiral could enforce his dog destruction order, he'd have to take up the captured weapons.

Confiscation began immediately. Each pistol, bayonet, and knife had to be logged in, labeled, and stored so it could be reissued before the men left the ship. The seizure process continued well past mid-voyage, at which time they had to start returning the arms to the soldiers. After all, with hundreds of thousands of troops waiting to come home, the ship was scheduled for an immediate turnaround; they couldn't waste valuable dock time returning souvenirs. The admiral conceded, and both mutts and men openly strolled the decks together.

The admiral and the ship's name have been lost to time. In 1998, I wrote a newspaper series about finding lost loved ones, which inspired me to locate Dad's driver so the old soldiers could reconnect. When I called Colonel Clifford Linley, I mentioned Dad's stories. Linley corroborated them but didn't want to discuss them further.

I believe the memories of Landsberg must have haunted Dad throughout his life. But always he had his own dogs to help him through his private pain. And while those French dogs saved the hearts and souls of his men during wartime, Dad simply returned the favor. For one week on a crowded troop transport ship at the end of the war in Europe, Dad had over a hundred dogs. That made young Lt. Rainbolt the happiest dog lover in the world.

Dog in the Nest

Dana Mentink

There would be no more dogs, of this, I was certain. With Nala, our beloved German shepherd, gone after twelve years, I was done with dogs, thank you very much. Nala, timid and starved when we got her, morphed into a seventy-pound bundle of devotion who quietly filled our home, the calm overseer of our chaotic little nest, my constant shadow.

But Nala's time had passed, and the Mentink nest, which had once been filled with the activity of fledgling girls, was cavernous and quiet. Now that there was no more clatter of Nala's nails on the floor, no more chiming of dog tags, the hush was deafening. Where were the babies that I fed and read to? The van full of girls and friends of girls and Girl Scout gear and musical instruments and tiny Barbie shoes wedged under seats with the odd Goldfish cracker and beaded bracelet? Where were those moments when they called for Mom to help with the dreaded science project or to shop for the party dress?

Where had the young birds who needed their mother gone? Though they still lived at home, they were shadows that drifted in and out, driving themselves to work and school, feeding and preening, singing their own songs. In the steady rhythm of days, with my eager Nala by my side, I had hardly noticed how adult feathers had taken the place of the soft down.

The chicks had grown up, so why the sadness? Hadn't they gone and done exactly what I'd prayed for? Fledged into independent women? Hadn't I asked God for this very empty nest, in a way?

But the answered prayer was more painful than I realized, and Nala was not there to quietly reassure me—no long walks to put the world back into order, the calming routine. Yes, there was work and chores and church responsibilities, but it felt like the nest was empty of the one thing that made it home . . . joy.

It was a great while before I felt the tug and peeked at the online photos of animals in need of homes. Big dogs like Nala, with fearful eyes and sad stories posted by the rescue groups. They needed someone, needed me, but still, I was unmoved. There would not be another Nala, and there would be no little girls to make soft blanket forts with a dog or hop around the yard in pursuit of a dirty canine in need of a bath. There would be no more Easter hunts requiring chubby human legs to outrun a canine who could sniff out an egg from a hundred paces. It would not be the same. But there were still the sad eyes in the photos and still the small tug from somewhere deep inside my soul.

Grudgingly, my girls and I went to the shelter to look at big dogs, shepherds, to look for Nala. We saw them, the sturdy, enthusiastic creatures, who sniffed and licked and wagged, but they did not look at me the way my Nala had. It had been a bad idea to try and fill the nest again, as if a strange dog could somehow restore things to the way they'd been before.

"Let's just look at this one. We won't take her home, just look," my birds chirped at me. A small dog, I sniffed. A yippy, fragile, half-crazed terrier mix. Exactly what I did not want.

We sat, all four of us, cross-legged on the cement floor that smelled of bleach.

"Juniper has been in two different shelters," the volunteer said, "and she's recovering from an illness. She has a bad knee. She will be shy, she will need some coaxing."

The pup, a cross between a slinky and a wire-haired terrier, scampered immediately to the first lap she saw, then to the second, and the third, and finally, to mine, accepting caresses and coos and adoration. It didn't take long to convince the young birds. I acquiesced, with an escape proviso.

"We'll take her home," I said, "but if it doesn't work out, she'll have to come back to the shelter."

The birds weren't listening as they argued over who would hold the nine-pound bundle on the way home, but back at the nest, the battle would begin. Round one . . . where would Juniper, aka Junie, sleep? Our thought? A crate in the kitchen. Her thought? Why not snuggle up in the bed with you fine folks? After three sleepless nights of ear-splitting whining, we compromised. A crate at the foot of our bed, using Mom's T-shirt as a security blanket. Détente.

Round two . . . potty training. This involved a battle of wills on a grander scale. The lines were drawn: stubborn adorable dog whom no one could be irritated with but me on one side, and equally stubborn momma who would not accept anything short of total surrender on the other. I tethered her to me, and we were on a ruthless schedule day and night. Tears, frustration, carpet cleaners, more exhaustion. "I will win," I told her. Finally, after two exhausting weeks, she replied with a twinkle in her brown eyes, "I will let you."

We have engaged in more battles that are, as of yet, no decisions. Junie is a plotter, a schemer, with a taste for Post-it Notes, my coffee, pencils, and the yard sprinklers. She finds me irrationally devoted to giving her baths and shushing her when she is performing her security duties by barking at the neighbors. I foresee more skirmishes ahead over Christmas decorations, the chewing of

Bibles, the worrying addition of Leaf Blower Man to the neighborhood, and whether or not it is acceptable to unzip Mom's purse and help oneself to the Kleenex.

So what has nine pounds of naughty in a fur coat done for me? She allows me to snuggle her close when she shivers in the winter cold, tucked inside my sweater, her wedge of a head nestled under my chin. For no discernible reason, she will sprint in madcap laps around the furniture until she exhausts herself, which fills the nest with rollicking good fun. Every morning she leaps from her bed on spring-loaded paws, steeped in the miracle of another morning, saying with her eyes, "How can you stand still when there is a whole new day unrolling just for you?"

Junie is a messy, naughty, joy-filled, curious, zany, pencil-chomping reminder that there is all the happiness and purpose and adventure that a body could possibly need waiting right outside that door. And most of all, Junie allows me to be a mother bird again, caring for her as she fills this quiet nest with noise and verve and joy, rescuing me from the silence and reminding me who I am.

My August Dog

Lonnie Hull DuPont

Recently one afternoon I curled up with my cats and took a nap. As I was dropping off, my mind meandered to the year I lived in Greece—a country where, as part of its culture, people nap every afternoon between two and five o'clock. They call this quiet time *mesimeri*.

I had never been a napper. It was the only issue my parents negotiated with me when I was a preschooler—that if I would lie down and try to nap, they'd let me stay up later that night. I remember the last day of those negotiated naps when my mother peeked in to see me looking back at her, wide awake as usual. She laughed and said, "Oh, just get up." I was never expected to nap again.

The year I turned thirty, I moved to Greece to stay one year in that beautiful land. I wound up loving Greek life—except, at first, *mesimeri*. It took ten months before I felt the least bit sleepy at the culturally prescribed time. Prior to that day, I took walks during *mesimeri*. The streets were deserted. The arid Greek heat didn't bother me—it was usually accompanied by an ocean wind, and it all felt good to me. I would walk through the streets where

I lived on the outskirts of Athens or climb the roads of the surrounding hills.

I never came upon other people at this time, but I often saw dogs. Even they took *mesimeri* on hot afternoons. Nondescript breeds, never chained or fenced, stretched themselves out under the shade of an olive tree, snoozing away the heat. In fact, I seldom saw a dog on its feet.

These walks gave me opportunity to reflect. I had come here following a hard time in my life—the sudden death of a man I loved very much. The loss had left me shattered and bewildered. American friends living in Greece encouraged me to come and stay with them as long as I needed. So I took a leave of absence from my job and prepared to be gone one year.

I arrived in Greece shell-shocked. While at home I had been keeping myself crazy busy so as not to feel my grief, in Greece I had nothing but time on my hands. Every day, all day, I thought about what had happened. I also reflected on how stressful my life had become, how rushed it was, and how obsessed I'd been with work.

By contrast, I observed that Greeks lived each day in a way that seemed more humane. They expressed their emotions easily. They took time for each other. They seemed to live in the present of each day. They moved slower—they slept in the middle of the day, for goodness' sake!—and they did all this with grace.

So I tried living the Greek way. I slowed way down. I spent time with people. Eventually my type A personality turned into about a C+. I started teaching conversational American-English to Greeks who planned to work in the States, and even that felt easy and light. Slowly I started to heal from my sadness and stress.

I wasn't sure how this new way of living would translate back home, and I did wonder about that, because over time, I truly changed. Then late one night while walking through Athens, I looked up at a stunning full moon and realized that I didn't have to go back to the frenetic way I'd been living. Ever. God had made a big beautiful world, and I wanted to know it. The next day, I wrote a letter resigning from my job.

I'd come to know a few American expatriates and US military people who wanted someone to house-sit during their excursions out of country. So for my last month in Greece, I moved into the tiny four-room house of an American couple I knew casually. I'll call them Mike and Beth, because I've forgotten their names.

When I checked in with Mike and Beth the night before they took their thirty-day leave, we sat in their kitchen. The back door stayed open to a small porch and a semi-walled yard. A young stray dog had been hanging around on the little porch. She was shy and nervous, and she clearly wanted to be taken in. They did not do that, but they did tolerate her presence, and they fed her.

The dog was very sweet, and I wondered why they made her stay outside. I was raised with dogs indoors, but it turned out neither Mike nor Beth had any particular affinity for pets or much experience with them. They did, however, let the dog stay, and they occasionally spoke to her as she watched them from the back door. They gave her a name that I felt was disrespectful to the dog, so I seldom used it.

Mike and Beth left for the month of August, and I moved into their house. They had been adamant that the dog stay outside the threshold of the open back door. But I really liked the dog, and I invited her into the kitchen to be with me. She walked in haltingly, tail sweeping the tiled floor, peeking up at me with hope in her brown eyes.

She was a shepherd mix, a little larger than a beagle, but thin—all the dogs in Greece seemed thin. She was a tawny blonde with a black nose, black feet, smiling black lips, and markings around her soft eyes that looked like excellently applied eyeliner. I used to pet her and tell her I wished I had such fine natural makeup on my own eyes. She would gaze up at me, smile her dog smile, and wag her tail.

45

For our time together, I renamed her. The Greek word for "child" is *pethi*. It's also an affectionate way to address someone, much like Americans might call even an adult friend "baby." The Greeks would add the word "my" (*mou*) to this endearment, and so did I. Now "my" dog was Pethimou.

I'd explain letting Pethimou in the house later on, but in deference to the people who really lived there, I asked her not to come into the bedroom. It was located next to the kitchen, and she co-operated without fuss. For much of the month we were together, Pethimou slept at my open bedroom door on the cool terrazzo hallway floor, her lovely black feet tucked in.

Many of my friends and students had escaped the August heat of Athens, so I was alone a lot that last month. But I had Pethimou, and she adoringly watched my every move. I was taking *mesimeri* by then, always with Pethimou sleeping nearby in the cool dark hallway.

One morning, I left my temporary pet on the porch with some extra food and water and told her I would be gone for a while but I'd be back. I'd been invited by friends to spend a couple of days sailing to the island of Aegina on a thirty-foot sailboat, and I didn't want to miss this. The boat's owner brought his Labrador retriever, one happy water dog on that rolling boat. I thought of Pethimou back at the porch and trusted all was okay.

It was a glorious and memorable weekend on the sunny Mediterranean, and I returned to the house wind-burned and weary. As I started up the back porch steps, I was suddenly met by a snarling, lunging dog.

Pethimou . . . ?

Indeed, it was my sweet dog. I backed down the stairs. Now I saw why she'd been abandoned. We hadn't seen she was pregnant, and while I was sailing, she'd given birth on the porch. No wonder she'd wanted to get indoors—she knew she would need shelter. I saw the puppy—only one—and understood why Pethimou was ready to attack. Momma Dog was protecting her baby.

I dropped my duffel bag in the yard and hurried to the house of a friend who had dogs. She grabbed some dog food, and we headed back to my place. "It's all right," my friend said. "The dog's nursing and she's extra hungry."

Sure enough, once the fragrance of that food came wafting out of the can, I had my sweet Pethimou back. Her tail wagged as she ate, but she still kept an eye on us. We made a bed for her and her baby in the corner of the porch, far enough from the door to allow me access to the house. My friend walked home, and I stayed on the back steps a while longer as Pethimou nursed her baby. "Don't worry, Little Momma," I said softly. "I won't go near him until you say so."

But oh how I wanted to! He had the coloring of his mother, but he was as fat as a piglet, not having to share any nutrients with other puppies. He snorted and wiggled, and I wanted to cuddle him in the worst way. I named him George after one of my students, a Greek doctor who soon would be moving to Chicago. Human George enjoyed that honor.

For the short time I had remaining in Athens, Pethimou, Baby George, and I were a family. Soon enough Pethimou allowed her son to waddle into the kitchen, and I had permission to hold that roly-poly little guy. I still have the strongest olfactory memory of his puppy smell. I wasted no time in finding someone who would commit to taking George when he was old enough. I didn't want him abandoned to the street like his mother once was.

I stayed at the house a lot those last weeks. After the sailing weekend, I had seen everything I was going to see in Greece. Now I simply wanted to enjoy the dogs and some solitude before going back to America. Pethimou and George and I took our *mesimeri* near each other every afternoon, shutters pulled against the heat.

During this time, I was also girding myself about returning home, nervous as to how I would handle it, considering how I had left it. As I worried, however, there was always a set of warm brown eyes watching me from the floor, even while she nursed George. I felt Pethimou somehow had tuned in to my increasing dread about leaving. The nervous porch dog was now a calm mother, and it seemed she was mothering me too. I could pet her and talk to her about everything I felt. She simply listened to my voice.

I flew home on the scheduled day. Before I left that morning, Pethimou and George joined me in the kitchen while I wrote a long letter to Mike and Beth, who would be back the next night. The people who wanted to adopt George confirmed it, so I left their name and number. I made sure my Greek neighbor would

Sprechen sie Deutsch?

Usually I train my dogs in English, but some I have trained to obey German commands. It never fails, when I'm doing a demonstration in my work with dogs, someone will ask, "Does your dog speak German?"

So why train in a foreign language? Police do it so a suspect can't command the dog. Likewise, handlers with protection-trained dogs may do the same. Some people do it simply because it is fun. I have a search and rescue dog who came from an abusive home where commands were given in English. I have retrained the dog with rewards and used German commands to eliminate the stress the English commands created.

If other members of the household aren't familiar with the foreign language commands, it can make it difficult for them to handle the dog. My poor husband wanted my dog to heel but didn't realize he was giving the German command to down. This is why my dogs are usually trained in English. Whatever language you choose to train in, as long as you are consistent, your dog will respond to your commands.

—Sherri Gallagher

feed and check on Pethimou on the back porch until Mike and Beth were home.

Then I wrote an appeal. I apologized for letting the dog in the kitchen but assured them she went no further into the house. I suggested they keep her. I had discovered she was a very well-mannered dog and would be good company—even some security—for Beth when Mike was on military maneuvers. But if they didn't want her, I begged them to please find her a good home. She was worth it. When later they wrote back to tell me they had decided to keep her, I was glad.

The last thing I did before I left Athens was spread one of my sun-faded cotton shirts in the doggie bed on the back porch. Right away Pethimou and George curled up on top of it. I petted them both for a long while and told them they would be all right. Then I went back into the kitchen and closed the back door. For the first and only time, I left the house via the front door. Later that day I flew back to America.

That was a long time ago. Today some of my best memories have to do with that fortunate year in Greece when I had the privilege to run away for a bit, to rest, and to change. I often see Pethimou's pretty face—it's as distinct in my memory as it was when I looked at her. I trust that in the end, I helped better her situation. She certainly helped me with mine.

There was something else. I began to see the surprise birth of her puppy just before I came home as an assurance that I would be all right—that I would have a rebirth of sorts at home like I had had in Greece, and that I would have a second chance at a good life without turning back into the stressed person I once was. That turned out to be true. God has been gracious. I am living the life I hoped to live.

And I nap now. I don't have a dog, but my cats slow me down and help me recharge, like Pethimou did during our August together in Greece.

A Magical Moment

Marci Kladnik

A decade ago, I was at a very low point in my life. I was permanently off work because of injuries and living alone with two cats and a dog in the tiny town of Los Alamos, California. Being the skeptic that I am, I hardly believed in miracles until one smacked me in the face in the form of Maggie, my Scottish terrier, and a feral kitten.

Having pets to care for when your life is falling apart keeps you grounded. Going through a life-changing event with cats is pretty low-key. As long as you don't forget to feed them (and they won't let you do that) and keep their litter boxes clean, they pretty much let you go through it on your own. They will come for their snuggles if they are that kind of kitty, but otherwise they will let you work out your own problems.

Maggie the dog, however, demanded her morning playtime even when I just wanted to stay curled in a ball on the couch. Her mission was to love me in spite of myself and to keep the day's routine going, including those daily walks. I couldn't resist that pleading look in her eyes or the way she'd bounce to the front door if I got off the couch for any reason.

One of these walks took me to the end of town on a sunny Sunday afternoon to visit a friend. A young woman named Linda was there, and my friend introduced me to her. Linda volunteered for a grassroots Trap-Neuter-Return (TNR) organization in Santa Barbara County but had recently moved away from Los Alamos. Now she was looking for someone to take over the feral cat trapping in town.

Linda explained how TNR controlled the street cat overpopulation problem. Adults were trapped, taken in for spay/neuter surgery, vaccinations, and flea treatment, and then released back to their territory. Any kittens young enough to socialize for adoption were removed to foster homes.

I was absolutely clueless about this cause, but having loved cats my whole life and having too much time on my hands (besides loving a challenge and desperately needing a distraction), I heard myself volunteer to be the new Los Alamos trapper.

"What about me?" I said. "I like cats!"

Done! Two nights later, Linda taught me the ropes. We were after a momma and her eight-week-old litter, three black kittens and one gray-and-white cutie, all still young enough to socialize.

The family was living in a series of three abandoned and falling-down shacks with two or three other adult cats. There was a woman in town who would come by daily with water and food, filling the bowls amidst the cobwebs and dust, careful to step around the gaping holes in the rotting floor. Faint sunlight filtered through the cracks in the walls and broken windows, and cats would peer down from the rafters and through the broken windows, waiting for her to leave. A few were friendly enough to allow petting, but the family Linda and I were after was untouchable.

That night of training netted the three black kittens. Linda took them immediately to a foster home in nearby Santa Barbara, leaving me to finish the job alone the next day.

51

My first night of solo trapping was a real coup. I caught the elusive mother cat and another black kitten, a fifth we hadn't known about. The little gray-and-white one peered at me from the rafters but refused to come down. Linda came to pick the mom and black kitten up; I would have to try again the next day for the last kitten.

Twenty-four hours later I finally had him. I quickly covered the trap to calm the frightened kitten and took him home with me. Too late to get him to the foster's and his littermates, I would have to keep the kitten overnight in my garage where it was warm, dark, safe, and quiet, all things comforting sans Mom.

In the morning, I tentatively lifted a corner of the sheet covering the trap holding the tiny feral kitten. Without warning, a bundle of gray and white fur, hissing, spitting and with wild slashing claws, flew against the cage. Now I was literally face-to-face with the reality of what feral meant. Feral kittens may be cute, but they aren't always cuddly!

"I don't like you either!" I muttered, pulling the sheet back, completely exposing the cage and its occupant. I had food to offer and a litter box to clean, but how to get close enough to do that without being attacked or the kitten escaping? He was terrified, backed into a far corner, shaking and mewing piteously. Still he spat and attacked if I came near. My heart broke for him even as I muttered those mean words.

As I wracked my brain for ideas to ease his terror, I looked the kitten over. He was a soft gray and white. A white saddle spilled over his shoulders down to a white belly and four white legs. Along his back was a faint sinuous dusting of white that snaked along his spine as though he had walked under a paintbrush. His nose was pink and his eyes were still kitten blue, having not yet morphed into their permanent color. How could I not love that sweet little face and want to cuddle the terrified baby, claws and all?

In my inexperience and naivety, I thought that perhaps if he saw me holding one of my cats he would realize I was no threat.

The kitten's mother was black, so I started with Dodo, who was also black. Then I tried again with Spencer. I carried the two out to the garage one at a time and held them up a safe distance from the cage. Both just hissed and struggled to get down while the kitten continued to shake and cry. I was at a loss.

Suddenly my dog Maggie popped into my head. *Why not?* I thought. *She likes cats.* Thinking back on it, though, holding up two cats and then a dog to a tiny, frightened kitten might not have been the wisest thing to do.

Scottish terriers, as a breed and by reputation, are often not fond of felines. Scotties were bred as vermin hunters, so it is in their nature to chase, dig, and kill, even animals as large as a badger or fox. Maggie was no different as she hunted gophers, mice, rats, and an occasional bird in the backyard. If it moved, she was on it.

But having lived with cats most of her life, she was an exception to her breed. She was gentle and motherly with Spencer when he joined our family as a kitten a few years before. And so I thought of my sweet dog while the poor frightened feral kitten cried his distress.

The moment I held Maggie up to see the kitten, the most astounding thing happened. They locked eyes, and the crying stopped instantly. Loud purring erupted from the tiny kitten, who began inching forward to push against the bars to get next to Maggie. I watched in shock. The little hairs on the back of my neck stood at attention.

Focused on the kitten with great interest, but not as prey, Maggie wiggled in my arms, obviously wanting to get a closer look. I stayed on high alert for any aggressive reactions from either animal as I slowly brought the dog in closer and let the two touch noses through the caging.

Not a hiss or a bark. And the loud rumbling purr never let up, not even when I tentatively put my finger into the cage to stroke the kitten's tiny side. I was still very leery of those claws and teeth.

I could see that the kitten desperately wanted to be with Maggie. Once again being foolhardy, I carefully opened the cage, gingerly scooped the kitten up, and gently placed him on my lap. He sat there, unrestrained and purring! The kitten paid no attention to me; he only wanted Maggie. The dog and I were both spellbound.

About ten minutes passed. I knew I'd just been witness to something miraculous, an instant taming of an extremely wild and frightened kitten by a Scottish terrier! *Did that really happen? Will it last? Now what do I do?*

I made a kitten nursery in the upstairs bathroom and moved the little guy into it. Maggie hovered close, sniffing the still-purring kitten from one end to the other.

Separating the pair for the time being, I went to fetch the kitten's mother from the veterinarian, as she had been spayed earlier that day. Since I had to keep her for two nights prior to releasing her back to the sheds, I put her cage in the nursery with the kitten. I made a little tent and bed against the side of Momma's kennel so they could be near each other.

Interestingly, the kitten did not purr when he saw his mother but broke into loud purring every time he saw Maggie. He would not even eat unless the dog was in the room. This was just fine with my Maggie, who hovered around to lick up the crumbs. The mother cat watched silently, as if even *she* sensed Maggie was special and no threat to her baby.

I really didn't want a third cat, but I realized the kitten/dog bond was so strong that I could not in good conscience break this pair up. I took the kitten in for his neuter appointment a week later. When I picked him up, I was handed a note from the vet regarding "Barn Cat." Now this kitten had a name, Barney, and I knew he was mine.

For eight years, Barney stuck close to Maggie. They napped together on the window seat and wandered the backyard side-by-side. Barney met us at the front door when Maggie and I returned from our morning walks. Barney always purred loudly in the dog's presence and rubbed along her side.

During those years, I continued trapping feral cats and fostering their kittens. Maggie and Barney teamed up to help socialize them, and it was a thrill to watch them in action. Maggie was a natural when it came to working with these skittish animals, and Barney took all his cues from his canine "mom," becoming a gentle welcoming soul himself.

So much magic happened on the window seat in my office that I could hardly write, as I was always reaching for a camera. Not only did Maggie and Barney tame scores of kittens, but the joy and love that this bonded pair brought to my life every day healed my heart. It also brought me a new career in writing and photography. It seems more than one miracle happened that day.

What's Wrong with Your Dog?

Susan C. Willett

Wh\hat's wrong with your dog?"

It was early fall, not quite sweater weather, with a slight wind that nonchalantly swept leaves along the path. Lost in my thoughts, I had stopped for a moment to let Pasha, my Keeshond mix, sniff at a clump of suspicious-looking weeds. Twelve years old, Pasha walked a little slower than he used to, but his tail curled smartly over his back, he still had a prancy bounce to his step, and he could be counted on to inspect every rock, bush, and tree along our route. A few blue jays flew overhead, providing raucous commentary.

What's wrong with my dog?

Two boys had come up behind me; I hadn't heard them approach due to the cacophonous jays. One kid wore the requisite hoodie uniform of eleven-year-olds, and the other had a football secured under his left arm.

I looked down to see what might be wrong with Pasha. He was still inspecting, his question mark tail stirring slightly in the breeze, his graying muzzle tucked deep into the plants.

"What do you mean, 'What's wrong?' He looks fine to me."

"His back," said Hoodie Kid. "What's wrong with his back? Does he have some kind of disease or something?"

Football scrunched up his face. "Eww."

Oh that.

The Keeshond breed has a double layer of luxurious fur, and Pasha certainly wasn't cheated out of that part of his inheritance. Yet on his back was a platter-sized bald spot, mottled bubble-gum pink and chocolate brown.

"He was hit by a car years ago. He's okay now, but he lost the fur on his back."

They looked unconvinced; maybe the dog had something contagious.

"Want to pet him? He loves when people pat him on his bald spot."

The two boys looked at each other. Neither wanted to appear grossed out in front of his friend, yet both weren't in a hurry to make contact with that awkwardly naked surface.

"Sure. Okay." That was Football. Pasha was finished with his business, and he looked up as both boys walked toward him. The dog wagged a greeting and offered a welcoming sniff.

"What's his name?" Hoodie softly brushed his hand across Pasha's back. The other boy set his football down as he kneeled next to my dog, who leaned toward them in anticipation.

Three wags later, the two boys were on the receiving end of soggy dog kisses, as they alternately ran their hands through Pasha's soft fur or gently stroked his bald back.

A scene like this played out often when I took Pasha for a walk, and I was nearly always caught off guard by the "What's wrong with your dog?" question and its variants.

Years previously, as my dog Kelsey—part shepherd, part collie, part hound, and part goofball—grew old, I opened my heart to the possibility that another dog would enter my life. I didn't go out looking and didn't visit local shelters—this was before the web and the concept of online rescue sites—but I was sure that the right dog would find me at the right time. So I waited.

And then he walked into my office.

A coworker had found a dog running around in a park near our marketing agency in a small New Jersey town. Though my coworker knocked on doors in the neighborhood, nobody recognized him or claimed him, and so she brought him to the office until township animal control could pick him up and take him to the shelter: an original Bring Your Dog to Work Day moment.

The dog's coat was luxurious and full; his pointed ears stood tall and attentive, and he seemed to crave attention. He was the friendliest creature I'd ever met, approaching every person sure in the knowledge that he or she was going to pet him and love him.

He was right. I wasn't the only one who fell in love with this marshmallow of a pup. The woman who found him wanted to take him home, but she already had three dogs, and her husband thought four was one too many. One of our tech people wanted to adopt him as well, but he didn't think his cats would appreciate a canine addition to the family. As for me, I called the animal shelter and asked them how long they waited to see if someone claims a dog before they put him up for adoption. Two weeks. I left my name and phone number, telling the shelter that if nobody showed up, I wanted him.

I called every other day, each time steeling myself for the moment when a volunteer would tell me how happy she was that the dog found his owner, although I selfishly hoped that wouldn't happen. I kept telling myself that if this were the dog I was waiting for, he would be mine. And if he wasn't, another would come along. Still, I counted the days, then the hours, then the minutes until the shelter opened on the fourteenth day.

During those two weeks, my colleagues—who shared none of my doubts on whether the dog would eventually come to live with me—pestered me daily: what was I going to name him? All I would say was that he reminded me of a Russian teddy bear—all fluff and comfort. Maybe an endearing Russian name, like Pasha? But I wasn't going to commit until I knew him better. Besides, I didn't want to invest my emotions in a name if it turned out he was not the dog I was waiting for, the one I was meant to have.

The minute the shelter opened on the dog's first adoptable day, I was at the door, brand-new leash in hand. He accompanied me back to work, where he made even more friends than on his first visit. Everyone stopped by my desk to greet him. "Hi, Pasha!" "Who's a good boy, Pasha?" "Pasha, I brought you treats."

By the end of the workday, Pasha was Pasha. He knew his name. And so it stuck.

I took him home, where he and Kelsey grew to like each other, playing and chasing and making sure the other dog always had the best toy, the best stick, the best food. Pasha turned out to be exactly what I saw the first time I met him—a teddy bear of a dog who loved to be hugged and fussed over.

When Kelsey died, my kids and I took Pasha for a long walk, re-tracing the route we usually took with both dogs, but now with only one. We all missed Kelsey, and it helped human and canine through our loss as we snuggled Pasha a little more, hugged him a little tighter, and petted him on his back in that special way that made him dance.

And then one night, Pasha chased a neighbor's cat into the street—oblivious to the car turning the corner.

The emergency vet told us he was very lucky; there were no broken bones, no internal bleeding. He was very badly bruised, but he would recover.

The night of the accident, I slept in the living room on the floor next to Pasha, propping him up when it hurt him to lie down, comforting him, and giving him the pain medication the vet had prescribed.

The next day, I noticed blood on Pasha's back. I gingerly moved his long fur aside to see what was bleeding. A clump came out in my hand, and underneath was angry skin, oozing blood. Every time I touched him, more fur fell out. It was time to call the vet. On the phone, my words tumbled out almost incoherently as I tried to describe the wads of blood-tinged fur that were falling off my dog.

"You'd better bring him in." Those words made me simultaneously relieved that Pasha would get the care he needed and scared that his injuries were worse than we had originally thought.

A vet tech took Pasha straight into the back while I sat on a hard plastic chair in the waiting room, staring blankly at the pictures of happy pets on the bulletin board. I checked my watch every few minutes to see that only seconds had gone by. The longer he was gone, the more insistently my heart pounded as terrible scenarios cascaded through my brain. After twenty real-time minutes inched by, the tech called me into the exam room. She closed the door and looked at me kindly, lightly touching my arm.

"He's okay."

I hadn't realized I was holding my breath until it escaped in a rush.

"But the vet wanted me to prepare you for what Pasha looks like now. When we shaved his fur to get a better look at his back, we discovered that the injury was . . . well . . . rather large. We thought it might be a bit shocking when you see him."

Even with that preparation, I gasped when Pasha walked into the room with the vet. Nearly half of his back was bloody and furless. He offered a sorrowful wag. My poor baby.

It took months of three-times-daily warm compresses, repurposed T-shirts to protect his back, three surgeries, and tons of love, but Pasha recovered—mostly. His fur never regrew; instead, our teddy bear dog now sported a huge pink and brown bald spot.

As for Pasha, once he healed completely, he enjoyed having people pat him on his bare skin. It must have been a unique sensation, without fur blocking a cool breeze or getting in the way of a loving caress.

For family and friends who knew Pasha, his naked spot was normal. My young kids and I would look at the patterns on his skin, finding images in the shapes we saw there. My daughter was sure one pink splotch looked just like Snoopy's pal Woodstock from the Peanuts comic strip. My son insisted another area looked like Australia. We'd pat the shapes and continents and watch our dog wiggle with pleasure. To us, Pasha felt very alive, as the warmth of his body was no longer trapped by the insulating fur.

In the summers, we protected his exposed area by slathering on sunscreen. The kids helped rub it in as Pasha danced with excitement; not only did the dog enjoy the attention and the back rub, but it meant we were going outside!

We didn't see anything missing when we looked at Pasha. We saw a whole dog whom we loved completely.

Which was why I was so clueless when anyone asked me what was wrong with my dog. I would patiently explain to people who thought Pasha was "ruined" and no longer beautiful, that he certainly didn't think so and neither did we; we were simply happy to still have him with us, having come so close to losing him.

Everyone who met Pasha and heard his story would eventually pet him—some more tentatively than others. He would respond the same way, with joyous sweeps of his tail and a soft nudge of his body, anticipating a gentle touch from yet another new best friend. The people would all take something away too. A lesson on beauty. A new perspective on disability. An acceptance of difference.

For the rest of Pasha's life, I continued to be surprised when someone asked me what was wrong with my dog.

Because there was *nothing* wrong.

Working Like a Dog

Sheryl Bass

It was my first day as communications coordinator of an international sandwich chain, and the work was already revolting. After nine months of unemployment and food stamps, I had taken the first job I was offered. All new hires were required to work in one of their restaurants for up to three weeks regardless of their position. Despite being a Jewish vegetarian, I spent my first day slicing and sorting ham.

After my three-week stint *serving* meat, I was to sit in a cubicle doing mental gymnastics trying to *promote* it. I had abandoned my principles for the almighty dollar. I attempted to scrub off the meat, grease, and my sullied values in a scalding shower. Then, I surfed the internet, desperately hoping to find a way out. My love of animals inevitably took me to the websites of my local humane societies. Though I didn't find myself a job, I might have done one better.

The Humane Society of Boulder Valley website featured an ad asking, "Is your pet a star?" I sat in front of the computer, thumbnail pressed to my lips as a smile slowly spread across them. I looked at my Chihuahua-Affenpinscher mix, Lyric, and asked her, "Wanna be famous, little girl?" She cocked her little black head to the side quizzically and wagged her tail.

In one week, she was to audition at the Boulder Dinner Theatre for the part of Toto in their four-month production of *The Wizard of Oz*. I called my parents and friends and asked them if they thought she could pass as a male Toto dog from the 1930s. I examined her round head, expressive brown eyes, long eyelashes, and pert little snout. From the dainty way she lifted one paw reluctantly when I walked her in the rain to the way she crossed her paws in front of her when she slept, she seemed about as masculine as Vivien Leigh in *Gone with the Wind*. Could she really impersonate a male dog? I decided to let the PetSmart grooming department increase her casting odds with a simple cairn terrier cut.

When we arrived at the Boulder Dinner Theatre lobby, I saw the director and immediately recalled the sting of rejection. Over the years, I had sent him several demo vocal CDs in an attempt to join his regular adult cast. He shook my hand as if he didn't remember me and offered Lyric a cursory pat on the head. Other dogs and their owners arrived soon after. Most of them were entirely wrong for the part. Many of them appeared to be more than thirty pounds—far too heavy for Dorothy to carry in a wicker basket.

A Humane Society trainer walked in and recognized Lyric and me from her "beginner," "advanced," and "tricks" classes. She and I nodded and smiled at one another.

A white curly-haired mutt sniffed a potted plant and lifted his leg. Just as I began to feel superior, Lyric toddled over to his fresh urine spot and added her own yellow brick road. One of the dinner theater staff rushed over with paper napkins and removed the mess as I covered my face with my hands. When I peeked through my fingers, Lyric looked inexplicably thrilled with her accomplishment.

The theater director looked on as the trainer asked each dog to perform basic commands. The director said he was concerned about the size of all of the dogs except for a black cocker spaniel and Lyric. To help Lyric win the part, I asked if I could demonstrate how she responded to both my verbal commands and hand signals. After Lyric was finished, the director clapped his hands and deemed her "brilliant." She was definitely a Toto, as was the cocker spaniel.

The cocker's mother and I were handed scripts so that we could run lines with our charges. We were told that each dog would do three or four shows per week for four months and would earn an impressive $40 per show. Our dogs would be independent contractors. However, we would have to complete the government paperwork in our own names (as canines lack social security numbers). He offered us days and times when the stage would be vacant so that we could go over scene blocking with our dogs.

It had been four short years since I adopted Lyric from the Denver Dumb Friends League. A Good Samaritan found her running down Federal Boulevard covered in her own filth and brought her to the shelter. Since then, I had painstakingly taught her to come when called, to sit, wait, release, kiss, and drop it. Now she was going to be a local star, and I felt like Professor Higgins in *My Fair Lady*.

Due to a scheduling conflict, I was unable to take Lyric to her first full cast rehearsal. Instead, I gave one of the stagehands a key to my apartment so that he could pick her up. Later that night, I received a call from an absolutely ebullient dinner theater director. He said that Lyric had such amazing instincts as an actor—that she even sat and placed her paw consolingly onto Dorothy's arm as she sang "Somewhere over the Rainbow." He said the other cast members watched this and cried. He reported that after Mrs. Gulch accused Toto of being vicious, Lyric deadpanned at the audience with the cutest pleading expression.

Then, he asked me if Lyric could play the part of Toto for the entire run of the show—to be the only cast member without an understudy. He added that the cocker spaniel didn't take direction very well. Lyric would make her salary and also be paid in prime rib and doting attention from the cast. He said that the stagehands could keep my house key and take turns picking Lyric up from home on days when I worked late. He said that since Lyric was so well behaved, I didn't even need to be at the shows to use hand signals and whisper commands to her from offstage. She easily obeyed commands from any cast member. Lyric's commitment would involve seven shows per week (no shows on Monday and two shows on Saturday), and the run was to be extended to five months. After a twinge of professional jealousy, I prayed that Lyric wouldn't get overwhelmed and said yes.

Though my corporate job was filled with gossipy coworkers, mind-numbing busywork, and countless ethical dilemmas, I cheered myself by counting the minutes until I could take Lyric to her next rehearsal. Initially, I worried that the food smells associated with dinner theater might distract little Lyric. I continued to practice with her from home with and without food distractions and soon got her to come when I called Lyric or Toto.

Finally, it was opening night. My boyfriend and I held our breath as orchestra music began to swell and hundreds of people took their seats. We both opened our programs and found that Lyric's "headshot" was in the playbill along with those of all the other cast members. The lights dimmed, and the young woman playing Dorothy arrived onstage holding my baby girl in such a way as to conceal her eight nipples. I heard the audience offer a collective "Awwww." I turned to a woman next to me and said, "That's my dog up there!" She smiled condescendingly and announced that her son was in the Lollipop Guild. Whatever.

Soon, the young woman playing Dorothy began to sing an introductory part of "Somewhere over the Rainbow" that in my thirty-three years on this planet I had never heard before. I wondered aloud why that part was not sung more often, as it was clearly the most touching of the entire composition. In essence, it tells of how we can feel hopeless in the rain until heaven offers us a rainbow of hope. It was as if Dorothy were speaking directly to me about my dismal career path versus Lyric's new opportunity.

As I watched the first act, I realized just how important Lyric's role is in this musical. Dorothy runs away from Mrs. Gulch because the old woman threatens to have the dog put down for biting her leg. Dorothy is angry at her aunt and farm staff for not defending Toto against these allegations and certain death. While on the lam, Dorothy sings to Toto of a place where she is understood and her dog would be safe. In context, this famous song is really a musical ode to the human-animal bond.

As the months progressed, theater reviewers from six daily area newspapers came to see the show and offer their opinions of the production. Most of the reviews were quite positive and some were more lukewarm, but without exception every publication mentioned Lyric by name in absolutely glowing terms.

I saw the show at least fifty times that summer and found a new life lesson in it every time. Eventually, I brought an ink pad with me and helped Lyric sign "pawtographs" after performances. Children and elderly folks eagerly posed with her to take commemorative photographs. Lyric was clearly making a difference to others.

I, on the other hand, was not. My meat-inundated restaurant experience had long since passed. However, my boss made me rewrite documents late into the night in what I eventually learned was an attempt to make me quit. Before Lyric's five-month *Wizard of Oz* run was over, I was unceremoniously fired. Needless to say, Lyric's more than $5,000 family contribution came in handy.

My rescue dog has since rescued me from countless bad jobs with her sweet, guileless example. She taught me that work should be nothing less than tail-waggin' fun. And on the very rare occasion when it's not, remember that there's no place like home.

A Racer's Second Chance

Kathrine Smith

I wanted a dog and was looking for a Jack Russell terrier at the time. Through my research, I had located a reputable breeder who had a kennel out of town. He raised and showed dogs and had several pet-quality terrier puppies available for adoption. I drove out to his residence and was quite impressed by the condition of his kennels and dogs.

This breeder had interviewed me for about an hour on the phone, pre-qualifying me as an adopter, before allowing a visit. He had asked me why I wanted a Jack Russell terrier. I told him I was drawn to the breed because of the TV show *Frasier* and the dog they called Eddie. Upon meeting and visiting with me in person, the dog breeder and professional handler quickly sized me up and said that he had another dog he wanted me to meet. Not a Jack Russell terrier. Not any kind of terrier at all. Not even a small breed dog. He wanted me to meet a massive greyhound he had found wandering on the side of a rural road. I couldn't believe it. I was not interested in adopting a greyhound. Or so I thought.

The moment I saw the dog, my heart melted. The man told me he was driving home late one night when he saw this greyhound on the road. At first, he thought it was a deer. But he quickly discerned that the huge beast in his headlights was a greyhound, and he stopped and was able to lure the dog to him with food.

The greyhound was severely malnourished and starving. He was an intact male dog, roaming a rural county road, confused and struggling to survive. The dog had tattoos in his ears, so the man knew that he was a racer and at one time had belonged to someone.

Before greyhound puppies are three months old, they are tattooed in both ears with the National Greyhound Association (NGA) identification numbers. No two racers have the same ear tattoos. The tattoo in a greyhound's left ear is his litter registration number, which is assigned by the NGA. The tattoo in his right ear identifies a specific puppy in that litter: the month and year of his birth and the order in his litter in which he was tattooed.

Based on this tattoo information, the man who picked the greyhound up off the road was able to find the dog's owner—who was located over a thousand miles away. The owner promptly requested that the dog be taken to a veterinarian to be euthanized. The greyhound had raced for several years, but when the dog was injured and could no longer race, the owner ordered his handler to kill the dog. For some reason, the handler couldn't bring himself to kill this specific dog, and somehow the greyhound ended up in rural Texas, a far distance from Florida, where he had lived and raced.

Thankfully, the owner agreed to surrender the greyhound on the condition that his name and kennel name would never be mentioned or contacted again. This was the early 1990s, before racing greyhound adoption programs gained popularity or support and other methods were used instead to dispose of dogs who could no longer race.

I remember feeling a profound sense of compassion as I looked at this magnificent former racer whose eyes had already seen so much. He was massive, with a spectacular color pattern of interesting bright orange patterns intermingled with black. He was considered a red brindle. His life had consisted of wearing a muzzle and chasing a mechanical rabbit around an oval track for the entertainment and amusement of people who only seemed to care about one thing: money. When I began talking to him, he bowed his head to me. This gentle giant. He wouldn't even look me in the eye. I knew that he was the dog I was meant to have, and I adopted him that day. So began a new journey with this greyhound I named Chance, as in second chance.

When it came to advice about rehabilitating a former racer, it seemed that everyone was an expert except me. I learned that greyhounds require a special dog collar, called a martingale, because sight hounds have narrow heads and slender, long, delicate necks, and can easily slip a regular dog collar off. A metal chain or prong collar is too harsh or harmful for the sensitive neck of a greyhound, and a slip collar can choke them. A martingale collar tightens slightly if a dog pulls on a leash, but not so much that it would choke the dog or harm his neck in any way. Many martingale collars are made especially for greyhounds, because the nylon material is wider, which provides greater comfort and support for both dog and handler.

Greyhounds are known as "sight hounds," and they can easily be incited to chase moving objects—any moving object is fair game for them. I also owned two very active rescue cats, and the other greyhound owners I consulted told me that a former racing greyhound would kill the cats. It would be too dangerous to house them together. I heard their concerns, and I realize these people thought they were looking out for me and my cats' best interest, but I figured that it was up to me to find a way—a way for a former racing greyhound to coexist peacefully with other animals, regardless of size or prey drive.

What most people don't know about greyhounds is that they are incredibly sensitive. Not only are they highly responsive to motion, they are also extremely sensitive to a pack leader, someone they respect. They are also very respectful of authority, when tempered with kindness, patience, and consistency.

The first serious lesson I taught Chance was the meaning of the word *no*. If he suddenly began to show interest in a cat, I calmly but firmly told him, "No." He would turn to look at me, and I would quickly follow up with, "Good boy!" He tested me at first, but within a few days, Chance knew that the cats were off-limits, and he never tried to chase or harm them in any way.

Chance was quick to learn, although he did present challenges, especially in the beginning. After living the life of a professional racer, he was incredibly serious and always so business-like. His doghood and puppyhood had been sacrificed for the sport of racing. He had lived to race, and raced to live. Now that he was no longer racing, it was like his life's purpose had been taken away from him. I had to teach him that it was okay to be a dog again.

At the time of adopting Chance, I also owned a beautiful Arabian mare named Ana Khianna. Like Chance, Khianna was also a rescue who had been successfully rehabilitated and was incredibly gentle. I often rode her bareback in open pastures or through dense woods, and we even swam across deep bodies of water together. She was a phenomenal horse.

I enlisted Khianna's assistance in helping me gain Chance's trust and respect in his rehabilitation process. I clipped a twenty-foot-long lunge line onto Chance's martingale collar and led him out to meet her. Khianna was accepting, but Chance didn't know what in the world to think about her. Every day for two weeks straight, I would ride Khianna bareback and lead Chance all over a hundred-acre pasture on that twenty-foot lunge line, with him by her side. At the end of the two weeks, I took the lunge line off Chance, and rather than run away, he stayed right by Khianna. We continued to work together to form an amazing bond of loyalty and trust.

I always wanted to give Chance the life that he deserved. I felt for him, because his life had always been so programmed and controlled and he had never been allowed to race on his own terms. When he'd suffered a serious injury after racing and winning for years, he was not allowed an opportunity to recover. His time was up. I wanted to give him his dignity back. I wanted Chance to live life on his terms now.

One day, when we were out in the pasture together, something happened.

Snap, snap! Chance tossed his muzzle up in the air, clapping his jaws in excitement.

"Do you wanna play?" I asked him.

Snap, snap! Chance clapped his jaws up into the air again, keeping his eyes steady on me.

"Chance, do you wanna *race*?" Then, the biggest open-mouth doggie grin you ever did see. My ole boy wanted to race me and my horse!

So I said, "On your mark . . . get set . . . go!"

And we were *off!*

Let me tell you something, that dog could *run*—and boy, did he ever smoke us! We were on a packed sand road that connected the hundred-acre property from one enclosed main road across to a second entrance. We raced across the entire stretch of pasture, and my horse and I didn't even come close to catching Chance. He beat us there and had already turned around to watch Khianna and me by the time we reached him. We were at a full run but couldn't catch this remarkable athlete.

There he stood, with the sweetest silly grin on his face, as if to say, "Hey there! Better luck next time—but you were a worthy opponent."

After that, I never went to the country without him. Chance was given the opportunity to race again, except this time on his own terms. He never had to wear a muzzle or chase a mechanical rabbit around a track. He no longer lived a regimented, programmed life, consisting of a cramped, prison-like kennel on a concrete floor, surrounded by metal bars, with many other greyhounds barking incessantly in their drab kennels. His days were no longer dictated by running to win money for his owner.

Chance lived up to his name from the moment we met, and we maintained a powerful connection. He went on to become certified nationally as a therapy dog (animal assisted therapy and activities) through the Delta Society Pet Partners Program, and he earned certifications through numerous pet therapy and activity organizations. He loved children, and they simply adored him. My gentle giant of a dog was calm and engaging, and he always bowed his head like a gentleman to be petted and loved.

Chance continued to race my horses and would eagerly engage them with his lighthearted, jaw-clapping double snaps in the air. The horses knew he was ready to run, and they obliged him. As a retired racer, he never lost a single race.

We all deserve a second chance at life, to love and be loved, and to thrive.

Chance reminded me every day of the incredible relationship we can all have and the lessons we can learn together—and to always remember that no matter what someone has been through, you can give them a second chance for a new life and redemption.

The Very Real Dog in a Make-Believe World

Tye Cranfill

At six years old I was convinced I was the only real boy on the planet and every other seemingly human person was simply a very convincing puppet. My parents and siblings were merely sophisticated marionettes that were manipulated by a highly skilled but invisible puppeteer. I often wondered why the puppet master had singled me out for the unique loneliness of being the sole human inhabitant of the earth. But there was no one to ask. Or, at least, no one to give me a straight answer.

"Just tell me the truth," I asked my older brother for about the hundredth time. "Are you just a puppet who is pretending to be my brother?"

Exasperated, my brother began making jerking, puppet-like movements with his arms and replied, "Why would you wonder that?"

I ran screaming from the room.

My mom was a more friendly puppet, but she nevertheless would never offer me a straight answer. How could she? She was simply having her strings pulled by the cruel puppeteer.

"Mom, can you tell me the truth and admit you aren't really real? Even though you are a good cook and you read to me, you are just a puppet sent to trick me. Can you just say it?"

"Honey, I am your real mom and this is your real family and none of us are puppets," she replied as she whipped up some brownie mix in a big Pyrex bowl. "Why do you ask such questions?"

"That's exactly what a puppet would say!" I fumed and stomped out of the room.

Many years later, a therapist opined that it was psychologically less painful to think of myself as the lone boy inhabiting the globe than it was to believe that the real people in my life could be so abusive and cruel. The ongoing sexual abuse by my uncle had created a deep rift in my mind. Viewing him as a cruel puppet—a nonperson—was the way my mind gave me at least some sort of protection. It is somewhat less painful to be used and abused by a malicious puppeteer than it is to be betrayed by someone you once thought loved you. And because my dad had out-of-control anger problems—with periodic but frenzied beatings for the most nominal of infractions—I certainly could not go to him. And my mother, trying to mentally survive her marriage, had adopted a policy of simply not seeing what was clearly visible.

So I think my therapist was right. It wasn't a healthy way to live, but being the only real human meant that at least I was not being abused by my real family. There was no real family.

There was, however, a real dog.

He lived next door and his name was Jack. He came over to my house every single day and spent far more time with me than he did with the little old lady who owned him. She was a fussy and preoccupied puppet, so Jack was free to adopt me. I think he preferred a real human, since he was a real dog. We completely connected.

I would lie out on the back lawn, and Jack would sit and let me talk to him for hours.

"We are in this together, Jack. It's like we are shipwrecked on an island. At least we have each other."

Jack would stare deeply into my young eyes, and I honestly believed he understood every word. They say that dogs can sense pain, and I had it by the industrial-sized barrel. I never spoke to Jack about the abuse exactly. In a way I still do not understand, I managed to simply make those frightening things go away once they temporarily ended. But I knew I was lonely and afraid, and I poured out that pain to Jack as he patiently listened to me every day.

"At least I have you, Jack. I don't have a mom or a dad or brothers or sisters. Just those fake ones, like the fake people at school. They're all just pretend. But you are real. I guess the puppet guy forgot about you. And it's a good thing, or I wouldn't have anyone."

I do not know what I would have done without Jack. He helped me bear the impossible load. He was the one listening ear in my entire confused and terrifying world. I really do believe God brought Jack into my life, because I had walled myself off from the rest of humanity. I desperately needed that dog, because at that point in my life I could not allow myself to trust another human being.

I will forever be a dog lover, and deeply grateful for each dog that has shared my home in the

> "People who rescue animals are basically angels, and the animals in return can really save *our* lives."
>
> —Tippi Hedren

years since my childhood. I don't recall the day that I stopped viewing the world as a place of fake people. It just kind of faded over time. And with a loving and very real wife, and kind people in a very real church, and the wisdom of a decidedly real and human therapist, I have experienced a level of healing that still astonishes me.

But I will never forget that a dog named Jack was a friend when I had no other friend, and he was my bridge to life when all other bridges had been burned. Grace comes to us in many forms—and sometimes even in the form of the lovable mutt next door.

Just the Dog for Us

Melody Carlson

Our beloved chocolate Labrador retriever, Bailey, had been part of our family for ten years when he passed away in the autumn. My husband and I felt totally blindsided by the heartbreak of losing him. We didn't think we'd ever want another dog. Who needs that kind of pain? But about six months after losing Bailey, I got a weird phone call from my mother.

The phone call was strange for several reasons. First of all, my mother (who is *not* a dog person) was calling to persuade me to "adopt" a dog. It was totally out of the blue, and I couldn't quite figure it out. But it got my attention because I'd been feeling a bit uneasy that day. Staying alone at our beach cabin, I'd just heard about some violent break-ins in our neighborhood. The idea of a dog companion suddenly had a slight appeal. Besides that, it was Mother's Day weekend, so I wanted to be extra nice to my well-meaning mom.

"I just know this is the perfect dog for you," my mother exclaimed. Okay, how she could possibly know this remains a mystery, but I took the bait. She explained that the dog was a "valuable purebred yellow Labrador retriever named Audrey." I think she was actually reading from notes. She then told me that the dog breeder involved with this "wonderful" dog was a friend from my mother's aqua-aerobics class. "And she and your cousin and I all agreed," my mother declared, "that this dog will be a perfect fit for you. You're just the one to rescue her."

Naturally this raised the question—*why?* If this dog was so valuable and perfect and wonderful, why did she need to be rescued? But my mother was rather vague about those details. Instead, she urged me to contact the owner as soon as possible. "I just know this dog is meant for you," she insisted before she hung up. And so, even though I still wasn't quite ready to give my heart to another dog, I promised to call the number.

After a lengthy and enlightening phone conversation with Audrey's owner—a man who dearly loved his dog—I learned that Audrey had been involved in a domestic dog situation where a beloved shih tzu had been on the losing end of a pet treat skirmish. The man's theory was that Audrey, who'd been raised from pup-hood with a pair of older miniature canine companions, didn't know her own two-year-old strength. "She'd simply outgrown them but didn't realize it." He sadly explained that when the bossy eleven-year-old shih tzu (the alpha dog of the family) snatched Audrey's doggie treat, Audrey simply yet eagerly attempted to retrieve it. Hence the unfortunate demise of the elderly shih tzu.

Audrey's owner disclosed that the deceased dog had belonged to his wife—and that she was deeply grieving her loss. As a result, she was unwilling to allow Audrey back into their home. Ever. Naturally this placed some strain on their relationship, since he adored Audrey. He went on to explain that Audrey, after undergoing thorough exams from the veterinarian, the doggie psychiatrist, and an expert dog trainer, had been pronounced perfectly safe. He also confided that she'd narrowly escaped "death row" and was currently lodged in the "Dog and Cat Hotel," which he confessed was not cheap.

Maybe it's because I'm a storyteller, but for some reason Audrey's sad tale intrigued me . . . and so we arranged to meet. It was hard not to fall for the energetic blonde dog. When I saw her big brown eyes, sweet innocent smile, and a golden coat that was softer than velvet, I was pretty much hooked. Just the same, I told him I'd think about it.

I went back to the beach cabin and discussed the possibility of re-homing a new dog with my husband. Chris was not quite as enthused as I was feeling. But when I mentioned the local news about a home invader in our beach house neighborhood, he was fully onboard.

The next day, after I quickly gathered some doggie supplies, Audrey's owner and I met up for the second time. And, feeling a bit nervous, I returned to the beach cabin with Audrey in the back seat. I suppose I felt a bit like a new mother. What if Audrey missed her previous owner? I could see that they'd been close. His eyes were misty as he'd said good-bye to her. Or what if Audrey was traumatized by her disrupted life?

But to my relief, we instantly began to bond. And Audrey seemed perfectly content. I quickly discovered that her favorite activity was to retrieve . . . anything. Balls, sticks, Frisbees, rotten apples. You threw it, she would fetch it. Again and again. This prompted lots of walks to the beach, a place we both love.

Not only that, but Audrey turned out to be a fabulous traveler. Unlike her predecessor (our beloved Bailey), who needed to stop every hour or so and sometimes got carsick, Audrey could make the entire three-hour trip to the beach, on winding roads, without a single stop. And she never whined or complained. And, perhaps her best trait was her surprising calmness—she was the kind of dog who takes everything in stride. Oh, she knew how to bark when someone came to the door, but other than that, she was very subdued.

Audrey quickly proved herself to be my faithful and protective companion. For those times when I was by myself, writing in the beach cabin, I always felt safe having her there with me. Even when I was startled awake at 3:00 a.m. in the springtime . . .

Audrey and I had been sleeping peacefully (Chris was out of town) when the howling sound of loud tsunami alarms split the night. I leaped out of bed and ran around, trying to figure out what to do next. Meanwhile, Audrey remained perfectly calm. I eventually grabbed my purse and keys and Audrey and got into the car. She was great company as I drove the evacuation route. Her calm demeanor was surprisingly soothing in the midst of that unsettling night. I began to realize that I probably needed her more than she needed me.

Even when Audrey was seriously injured while retrieving a thrown stick on the beach (something we never do anymore) she remained perfectly calm. Although the stick had painfully punctured the roof of her mouth, resulting in the loss of one eye's vision, she was still able to calmly walk the two miles back to the cabin with me. And even though I was a wreck while I impatiently waited for the vet to see her, Audrey simply settled down on the floor, calmly waiting.

Audrey will be ten years old this spring, and although she's showing her age, she's still healthy, energetic, and happy, and she is still blessedly calm. She has a bed in my writing studio and is always eager to "go to work," which basically amounts to her sleeping while I'm writing. But Audrey still shows us that, even in the midst of the chaos that occasionally happens in our lives, she knows how to keep her cool.

So I have to admit that my mother was right after all—Audrey really was just the dog for us. She needed us to give her a second chance at a good home . . . and we needed her to give us a second chance at giving our hearts to a sweet dog. And I'm glad we did!

Two Rotties and a Toddler

Wanda Dyson

We're taking in two more dogs tomorrow. A pair of rottweilers."

I stared at my husband in disbelief. Our foster kennels were full, and I had my hands full trying to cope with the needs of our little girl, Jayme, who, at the age of eighteen months, had stopped talking. "We agreed no more dogs until most of what we have are adopted. I'm meeting with doctors three days a week as it is. I don't have time to work with more dogs."

Jim stroked his beard, looking out the kitchen window instead of at me. I knew he was hurting as much as I was about our baby. "The doctors have spoken. There's nothing more that can be done except teach her sign language. Let her go to that special school. It's the best thing for her right now."

I wiped Jayme's face and tried to feed her another spoonful of applesauce. She turned her head. "How can she be talking just fine one day and not speaking at all the next?"

He shook his head as he turned and leaned back against the counter. "I don't know, but we've seen enough doctors. They all say the same thing. She's severely autistic, and that's not something that can be cured."

"So we give up and just send her off to a special school."

"We aren't giving up or sending her away! The bus will pick her up, and for five hours a day, experts will work with her, teaching her sign language so she can communicate with us."

I knew he was right. Two days later, Jayme started going to a special school for disabled children, and I went back to working with the dogs while she was at school. We had a chow, three bichons, an Irish setter, a mixed-breed terrier, and two Dobermans.

Jayme was not thriving in the special school the way everyone had assumed she would. In spite of her highly qualified teachers, Jayme was not making the connection between sign language and communication. After two weeks she had yet to learn even one word. Frustration was running high for all of us but perhaps Jayme most of all as she struggled every day to make her needs and wants known.

In the meantime, the two new rottweilers, Crowbar and Sagie, were a delight to work with. Neither was aggressive, both thought they were big lap dogs, and both proved to be extremely smart. The paperwork that came with the dogs indicated that they were housebroken, they were voice and hand-signal trained, and that Sagie had a problem with other dogs. It was my job to take them through all their paces and work with them on problem areas to make it easier to find forever homes.

During Jayme's third week at her special school, I was working the two rotties out front. I watched for Jayme's bus as I ran the dogs through their paces. I went from voice to hand signals and back again, commanding first one, then the other, then both together. We were hoping that they would remain together in their forever home since they'd grown up together.

Leaving Crowbar in a sit-stay about twenty feet in front of me, and using hand signals only, I commanded Sagie to heel and then sit at my side. I didn't notice that Jayme's bus had arrived. The aide on the bus was standing at the gate with Jayme, watching in fascination as I put the dogs through their paces. I lifted my hand, and Crowbar stood up. Then I silently commanded him to approach. Stop. Sit. Down. Stand. Heel.

The bus aide started applauding. I put both dogs in a sit-stay before running over to the gate to get Jayme. "I'm so sorry. I didn't realize you'd arrived."

"We were having fun watching you."

I opened the gate and took Jayme's hand. "Thanks again."

"How did you teach those dogs to do that?" the aide asked.

"I wish I could take credit, but they had excellent training before they came to me."

"Why would someone give them up?"

"A young couple bought them, trained them, loved them, and then had a baby. They found out that two adults, two full-grown rottweilers, and a newborn baby don't work well in a one bedroom apartment."

"I can see that. Shame though. They're beautiful."

"They are. We already have a long wait list on them, but we're holding out for a bit to see if someone wants both of them together."

"Well, I wish I could take them but my husband doesn't like dogs." She waved and walked back to the bus. "See you tomorrow."

I waved in return and then turned my attention back to my daughter. She stood with both rotties sitting in front of her. Giggling, she made a little sign with her fist, and both dogs dropped into a down-stay. Jayme giggled again and made another sign.

My heart jumped up into my throat. She got it! She'd made the connection between forming a shape with her hands and communication. She was "talking" to the dogs, and they were responding!

I felt like dancing across the yard! What experts and parents couldn't do, two dogs had managed to do. They reached across a nonverbal barrier and touched the lonely, frightened child and made her smile again. As far as I was concerned, those two dogs had a home for life.

Two weeks later, that issue was pretty much settled.

As Jim and I cleaned the kennels, Jayme sat on the patio playing with her Matchbox cars. I went to move one of the dogs to a clean run on the other side of the house. My husband went inside to replace a broken hose fixture. When we both returned, we found that our daughter was gone.

We searched the yard, the house, and then the street out front when we discovered the front gate wide open. Jayme was nowhere in sight. How could a child on such short legs move so quickly?

As panic began to settle in, I went up one street and my husband another. Still no Jayme. Ten minutes. Twenty. Still no sign of our daughter.

Jim was on the phone with the police when a pickup truck pulled up in front of our house. "You folks missing a little girl and two dogs?"

Jim ended the call. "Yes."

"She's two streets over behind you in our sandpile. Our masons don't mind her. She's just playing with a Matchbox car, but she has one rottweiler on one side of her and one on the other side of her, and as long as my men keep their distance, those dogs are just fine. But if anyone gets too close, they both stand up and show teeth. I think they mean business."

How she managed to get to the construction site will forever be a mystery, but the love and the special bond that had grown between our little girl and these two dogs was nothing short of a miracle. Crowbar was with us for nearly ten years before he finally passed on, and Sagie went just a few months after Crowbar. As much as they both loved Jayme, I think Sagie found it too difficult to go on without her life mate.

Many dogs came and went over the years, but Jayme never took to any of them the way she had with Crowbar and Sagie. About a year after Crowbar's death, Jim was at a yard sale with Jayme. She stopped in front of a large black velvet painting of a rottweiler, and she looked up at her dad and smiled. "Bah."

While it wasn't actually a picture of her Crowbar, it did look an awful lot like him. "That's not Bar, honey."

"Bah," she insisted.

Yes, Jim bought her that painting of her "Bah."

The Island Dog Who Refused to Give Up

Leanne Southall

When we were in our thirties, my husband, Scott, and I lost our Manchester terrier, Wicket, to lymphoma. Our house felt strangely empty without her wagging around our feet. We wandered through our house in Toronto, no longer feeling at home. When friends offered us their vacation condo on the Caribbean island of St. Martin, we gladly accepted. I was still grieving. I was also six months pregnant, and a week in the Caribbean sounded like the rest and recovery we could use. We needed to establish a new normal.

From the moment we got off the plane on the island, I barely noticed anything but the stray dogs. They were everywhere. Judging by the locals' casual demeanor, this was the way of the island. The strays were skittish and skinny. And there were oh so many.

Sitting down at a local restaurant for our first island meal, I glanced at the menu. Despite the many vegetarian delicacies, I had no appetite. I ordered a bowl of pasta marinara. A simple dish of spaghetti noodles in a white bowl was placed before me. I forked it. I spun it. I twirled it. I could not eat it. When Scott finally asked why I wasn't eating, the floodgates opened. Tears poured into my pasta. How could I—who had already had breakfast and a snack—eat another meal while a stray dog waited outside for the end-of-the-night garbage takeout? It was all entirely absurd.

Scott paused, his forkful of food midway to his mouth. The waiter came over to check on us. Neither of us was eating, and I was crying. Scott reassured the waiter, "Yes, everything is excellent. Thank you." Poor confused waiter.

We packed our meals to take out. Now that the decision had been made, not a moment could be wasted; I had to get to a dog with our food. We quickly and carelessly crossed the busy street to feed a dog who was not going anywhere anytime soon. I opened takeout containers, tossed them toward the dog, and backed away as she ate. Temporary relief for me, sustenance for the dog.

That evening was the beginning of a seven-day struggle to enjoy a meal ourselves without guilt. I perused menus for foods that would be gentle on a hungry dog's tummy. Our meal routine was to order extra, pack it up, and find a dog.

And did we ever find a dog!

The night before our return flight to Canada, we were headed back to the condo. We had spent some time driving around the circumference of the island during those lazy beach days. But now Scott made a wrong turn. We drove half a mile along a sparse residential stretch to an eventual dead end overlooking a breathtaking town. There was unspoken nervousness about the turn we had to make to get out of the tight dead end. Scott is a superb driver, and I exhaled with relief as we safely headed back to the main drag. It was then that I saw something out of my passenger window.

My eyes caught a very quick blur of an emaciated dog, standing yet slouching with his head hung so low, he looked like a stegosaurus. We had encountered so very many homeless dogs during the previous seven days. But this dog's image was all I could see as we continued to drive along. I described to Scott what I had seen, and tears became sobs. "Please, let's go back," I said. We both knew it was the only thing we could do.

I felt both relieved and anxious for what was to come as we turned the car back around. Having been around the small island a number of times that week, we had noticed veterinary offices here and there. As we headed back to the street where I had spotted the dog, we approached a green trailer on wheels off to the right. A sign simply read "Vet." We parked. I ran up the three metal steps hoping that what looked like a closed business might be mercifully open. The door was locked. It was 8:00 p.m.

We returned to where the dog had been. It was gone, of course. And our flight back to Toronto was at 11:00 the following morning.

Without needing to say much to each other, we drove back to our condo. I searched online for a vet, whom I'd call the following morning. Determined to find the dog, we intended to make arrangements to . . . well, we didn't know. But something needed to be done; it was intolerable that an animal could suffer day after day simply because it couldn't get itself to a vet.

It was a near-sleepless night as I talked to that dog in my mind. "Just one more night. Just hold on for one more night, and we'll help you."

Scott made a bowl of pasta in the morning, all that was left in the condo mini-kitchen, and we picked up a baguette sandwich at the local bakery. We had two hours before the rental car was due at the airport. In silent determination, we packed our suitcases into the trunk. The fact that the chances were slim that we would ever find this homeless dog again didn't cross my mind anymore. Throughout the night, I had prayed and truly believed we would find the dog.

We drove off, a steaming bowl of pasta and an open-faced baguette on my lap. We turned onto the wrong-turn road from yesterday, my stomach doing flips. Scott slowed down as we began our search of the area. The car was hardly stopped when I pushed open the door and jumped out. There it was!

That gray heap of a dog was hiding under a blue parked car on this dusty road. I approached ever so slowly, crouched low and sideways, trying to look nonthreatening. In a high voice like a sweet momma would sound, I whispered, "Good boy, good girl." Then recalling that this part of the island was French-speaking, I whispered in my third-grade French, *"Bien garçon, bien fille."* I then realized that this dog had likely never heard "good" anything before.

I held out the pasta bowl in one hand and my bikini-strap-turned-noose-leash in the other hand, ready to gently take hold of this poor dog. Finding this homeless dog was a huge triumph. It would be utter defeat if I did not manage to get the dog to come to me for help.

But he did. He crouched ever so slowly toward me. Perhaps the idea that I could be a threat wasn't the biggest concern for this poor soul; the risk would be worth it for the food. He came close and put his head in the bowl. I slowly, breathlessly placed the makeshift leash around his neck. Scott had driven up quietly and opened the back door of the car.

The condition of this dog, seen up close, rendered us speechless. He had no hair on his body. His scarred gray skin was a mess of scabs, pus, and blood. His entire body was surrounded by a cloud of bugs and mites of all kinds. The flying bugs swarmed his entire body, as if they owned him. Ooze discharged from his eyes, nose, and even his penis. He was bone thin and so very weak.

But those beautiful brown eyes . . .

We hoisted him into the back seat with me. As Scott drove to the vet's address we had scribbled on a piece of paper, I spoke soothingly to the dog. When he turned his head toward the back window, he smacked his head against it. He had probably never been in a car before, and he didn't understand windows. I reassured this poor dog that this last bit of extra stress would be worth it.

We carried him into the veterinary hospital entrance. We must have been a sight when we entered because the staff ushered everyone out of the way, clearing a path to the back. We laid him, accompanied by the bugs, onto the table. The vet appeared immediately. Scott and I joined the staff surrounding the dog while the vet examined him.

No one said a word. Not about money. Not about how this happened. Not about where he came from. Not about who we were, not even our names. Everyone was silent.

While we knew this might be the end for the dog, we also knew that this degree of suffering was no way of life. The dog did not flinch while he was poked, prodded, and pinched. The vet took a scraping from the dog's inner ear flap; the dog gazed passively into the vet's eyes. On occasion, we all caught ourselves glancing up at one another in disbelief. I had worked in veterinary hospitals for years, but it amazed me and everyone present how trusting this dog was. He gave himself over completely to our hands.

The vet finally spoke, showing us the dog's mouth. Most of his front teeth were completely ground down to the gum from trying to gnash the itchy bugs away. There were exposed nerves and an abscess in his mouth. Infection was obvious, given the oozing discharge. He was malnourished, evident by a complete lack of hair and a body reduced to skin and bone. At some point, he had experienced a physical trauma, which resulted in the visible scarring on his hips and belly.

His heart sounded good; distemper was rampant on the island but—thank God—his skin scraping proved negative. After a thorough exam, the vet told us that this dog's injuries were for the most part external, nothing that medicine and food and love couldn't fix. And maybe a little dental work.

We were over the moon! A second chance at life!

We offered to pay his vet bill to make this dog whole again. We explained that our flight to Canada left in just over an hour. So, if the vet would kindly deliver the dog to a shelter when he was well enough, we'd compensate him for his trouble.

This was met with a long pause. The vet explained that there were no shelters on the island. He could care for the dog until he was well, at which time he would have to release him to the street.

Or, the vet said nonchalantly, the dog could see snow someday.

I was confused. Why was the vet talking about snow at that tragic moment? Scott, however, knew exactly what the vet meant. This dog could be ours; when he was healthy enough, he could fly to Canada and join our family.

What about that split-second moment I had glanced out of my passenger window? Was I meant to see him? We couldn't leave his survival to chance. No longer would this dog be on his own. He deserved a family. Everyone needs to be loved.

Three weeks later, the dog was healthy enough to travel. The vet put him on a plane to New York, and I picked him up at JFK Airport. I drove him across the border into Canada and to our home.

It was incredible to see what love and medicine can do to turn an animal's life around so quickly. For weeks he slept with our hands on his chest; we lavished him with gentle, consoling touches and words. He began to bark and bounce. His hair began to grow in, which is when we learned he was actually black. And he loved the snow!

His name, of course, is Martin, a tribute to his birthplace. We call him Marty (sometimes Marty-pants). He now lives with us in Los Angeles with our daughter Morgan, who was born three months later.

He is an island dog through and through—super chill. And he loves lying on the black asphalt in the middle of our quiet cul-de-sac. Still a street dog, yes, but a much happier one.

Part of the Solution

Sherri Gallagher

All it takes is one ring.

Having a child away at college meant that a phone ringing late at night would cause an instant adrenaline rush. My husband was still up and had answered on the first ring, but that one ring was all it took to bring me fully awake.

Flinging the covers away, I dove for the stairs, not bothering to turn on a light. This resulted in my tripping over Lektor, my search and rescue (SAR) dog standing guard at the head of the stairs. German shepherds are herding dogs with an instinctive need to know and control the movements of their pack. So they have a habit of sleeping at traffic control points like the head of stairs. I knew it was Lektor's usual spot, but his dark sable coat prevented me from seeing him in the night.

A quick grab of the railing kept me from a sliding header down the stairs. The sharp jerk to my arm reminded me to think before acting. One of the SAR team mantras ran through my head: *Be part of the solution, not part of the problem.* If my foolishness had gotten me injured and the call was about our son, my husband would have had to make the difficult choice of whom to help first. That would have made me part of the problem.

I clambered to my feet, trying to make out my husband's words. By the time I had my balance, I understood that our son was fine. But I also knew someone else's child was in trouble, the kind of trouble that needed a canine search and rescue team.

I headed back to our bedroom to change. It was 10:30 at night. Temperatures were in the low forties, and there was a deluge of rain outside. Whoever it was, the odds of them being dressed to survive in this kind of weather were slim. That meant minutes could make the difference between a shivering subject or one dying from hypothermia.

Lektor sensed we were going to work and began pacing the room. I was pulling heavy wool socks on over my thermal liner socks when my husband appeared.

"What have we got?"

He grabbed a turtleneck out of his drawer and spoke through the fabric. "A potential suicide."

"Where?"

"Will County, on the outskirts of Joliet."

That was bad. We had a couple of hours of driving just to get to the search. "Is the Will County Emergency Management Agency activated?"

"That's who called. At least we won't need the base camp."

Usually when we took search calls, we went as a unit. My husband would handle liaison, assigning resources, and communications. We had an old bread truck fitted with computers and mapping programs, radios, cooking equipment, and survival gear. The team used it as a base of operations. We would drive to the base camp, and handlers would follow with their dogs in SUVs.

"I'll grab our gear." I headed for the door, only to have my way blocked once again by Lektor. I pulled his scruff to move his ninety-eight pounds of muscle and bone out of my path. I added some mock exasperation to my voice. "And the dog."

It took less than ten minutes to get our big diesel Excursion loaded. We pulled out of the driveway and rolled swiftly through the darkness, rain hammering on the windshield. I'm not fond of night driving, and I like it even less in the rain. But my husband handled driving in any condition like a long-haul trucker. A little rain and darkness were no big deal.

Volunteers for SAR take on hard, demanding work with constant training and focus, all without pay. So search teams go through an ebb and flow of people. To train a fully qualified dog and handler usually takes two years. Generally it takes longer to train the handler than the dog. Between first aid and ham radio licensing, map and compass and GPS training, plus learning to read and train a dog, not to mention physical fitness testing, the attrition is high.

We were currently at an ebb in our team's cycle. For the time being, Lektor and I were the only fully operational dog and handler team available. Others were in training but not ready for searches—and certainly not for a night search, the most difficult and dangerous search of all.

I watched my husband's face illuminated by dash lights. "How long has the subject been gone?"

"Between six and eight hours."

"It would be nice if we were activated in daylight once in a while," I whined.

"Agreed. In this case, it took a while to get a last known point. They just found her car in a grocery store parking lot."

"What do we know about her?"

"She's in her forties, brown hair, blue eyes, about five-five, and 150 pounds. No description of clothing, but probably jeans and sneakers. She's been depressed, but doctors thought the meds were working. She lives alone. Her mother checks on her daily and found a note from her, apologizing for being such a drain and promising not to be a problem anymore."

I felt an instant chill. Suicide was a distinct possibility. "That could mean a lot of things, not just suicide."

"Yes, but she has tried it in the past."

My husband's comment silenced me, but I shook off negative emotion. I would be part of the solution. Until we found her, as far as we were concerned, she was alive. "How many dogs were they able to call?"

"Just Lektor."

My heart did a stutter. We were the only canine team on the search? Okay, I know one dog is more effective in an air scent search than a hundred people, but still . . . just us? What if we messed up? What if Lektor had a bad night? Dogs are living creatures who have good days and bad days. Would I be able to read my dog in the darkness and rain as he blasted past on his looping search for the missing human?

I looked to the back seats. Lektor lounged in his crate, eyes calm but alert. His big ears were up and swiveling as he picked up on the emotional currents flowing around inside our vehicle. He panted a slow, steady rhythm, his pink tongue moving in time to his heartbeat. No yawning or stress markers; basically he wore the equivalent of a canine smile. My nerves steadied. He was ready to work.

My husband glanced over and smiled at me as I spun forward. "You'll do fine. You're the best dog and handler team I know, and I know a lot of them. We've got a couple of hours, so try to sleep."

How did my husband always know what I was thinking? I closed my eyes and used breathing techniques to try and still the adrenaline and worry that came with every call for help. Sleep escaped me, but at least I rested my muscles.

The search was being run out of an RV, the area surrounding it lit by floodlights while generators filled the night air with noise and fumes. Rain still fell. Each drop looked like a streak of light in the night sky until it collected and formed puddles on the pavement.

Twenty-five ground searchers had been deployed by the time we arrived. We checked in to the command center.

The incident commander spoke without looking up from his forms. "Thank you for coming. We need to see if the dog can give us a direction of travel from the subject's vehicle."

My first thought was, *You want what?* Thankfully I was too startled to speak.

Lektor had been trained to track on the ground, but he hated it. He was a great air scent dog, covering huge areas efficiently, but tracking was not his strength. In addition, they wanted him to track on a hard surface that did not hold scent well and had been rained on for hours.

"Sir, I am willing to give it a shot, but the probability is low that there will be any scent left to follow."

He finally looked up. "If you can't track, why did you come?"

"We're usually called out for air scent."

He stood and motioned to another man holding a slim jim to open the locked car. "Well, tonight you get to track. Get your dog."

I'd taught Lektor to track using a light harness that was a slender strip of leather running from his collar between his front legs to a strap around his waist. The ten-meter leash hooked to a ring on the waist strap and ran back between the dog's rear legs. It was lightweight enough not to interfere with Lektor's movement. With this configuration, it was almost impossible for a handler to steer or direct the dog, and that was important. If he could find a scent, Lektor had to tell us where the subject went instead of me guiding him where I thought the subject would go. Humans are notoriously wrong about these kinds of things.

The man with the slim jim swiftly opened the door and stood back. Lektor hurried over to the driver's seat and looked in.

"Take scent," I commanded, then pulled him back out of the vehicle with the German command to track: *"Suche."*

Lektor dropped his nose to the ground, swinging his head from side to side, and then proceeded down the side and around the back of the car. I fed out the line as smoothly as I could, watching to see if he would raise his head or give me any indication he had lost the scent.

He moved at a steady pace, never lifting his head, although the tilt of his ears told me he was shifting from footprint to footprint. Right, left, right . . . My dog was actually tracking in impossible conditions. I followed, attached to the leash handle ten meters behind my dog. My husband and another team member followed behind me.

Across the parking lot we went, then across the entry road up to the door of a pharmacy. Lektor sat and looked over his shoulder as if to say, "Hey—open the door."

I know a grin lit my face. I could hear my husband calling the incident command and asking if they wanted us to confirm if the subject had been at the store. We were directed to continue searching.

Once again, I pulled Lektor back and gave the command to track. He dropped his nose to the ground and led us around the front of the building. Lektor took us past a Burger King without so much as a pause and straight to the door of a McDonald's.

I restarted him while the men behind me called in the new information. Lektor took me directly to an ATM and then headed across a wide, plowed field. Once in the muddy dirt, he pulled harder, wanting to go faster. Clearly the scent was stronger. His powerful paws threw up clods of dirt in his desire to move more quickly while I used my weight and popping corrections to slow him. Speed can be the enemy of a tracking dog. In the rush for forward progress, it is easy to pass a turn and lose the scent. My job as handler was to keep the dog motivated to move forward but not to move so fast he'd miss a turn.

We emerged at a light post. Lektor stopped and sat, panting. I hurried to water my dog. His body language was clear. The scent trail had ended. But why here? As Lektor lapped water from my hydration pack, I could hear my husband on the radio.

"The canine is indicating the loss of scent at the bus stop on . . ."

I looked at the light post. Sure enough, a bus stop sign hung there. I gave Lektor a hug before turning to my husband. "Now what do they want us to do?"

"Clear the fields between here and the construction site and then the construction site itself."

"Awesome." I swiftly removed the tracking gear and put on Lektor's light-up collar and SAR vest. After checking the wind direction, I gave the command my dog had been shaking with excitement to hear: "Go find."

Lektor launched into the darkness, becoming a blinking blue dot looping out and around us as he searched and clearly indicated that the farm fields lacked anything with a human scent. My dog would have told me if he found so much as a gum wrapper, but his steady sweeps told me nobody was lying in the mud.

Lektor scrambled in and out of foundations and under equipment trailers at a lope, as if daring us to follow. As a small woman, I didn't have trouble following his lead in the tight spaces except when the forty-pound pack I wore got caught. The comments of the big men trying to keep up with us told me they weren't having as easy a time of it.

It was five in the morning when the call came in to cease and return to base. In the debriefing, we learned the woman had indeed gone to the drug store and the McDonald's. Incident command had not contacted the bank. However, they had pinged the subject's cell phone, and it was on a bus in Kentucky.

It had taken most of the night to confirm she was actually with her phone. One searcher had fallen and broken a leg, and another was waiting at the emergency room with a possible sprain. But these were common risks of searching in the dark. We had all known the risks when we agreed to come out, and no one gave their injuries a second thought. We found a live subject, not a suicide victim, so this was a good search. After the debriefing, we were all thanked for our efforts and released.

The rain had finally stopped. I rubbed a towel down Lektor's thick coat. It had done exactly what God designed it to do—cast the water off the top fur while the downy undercoat that gave the breed the nickname "German Shedders" stayed dry. Lektor hopped up into the crate and relaxed, panting hot breaths that fogged the windows. Climbing in the back while my husband stood guard outside, I stripped my rain-soaked clothing and changed into dry jeans. My husband preferred to stay dressed and crank the heat to dry himself.

We started the long trip home. Lektor slept as my husband drove us safely through the ever-decreasing darkness toward the rising sun. I drifted off to sleep, knowing this time I had been part of the solution.

Surrender

Lisa Begin-Kruysman

On a dreary damp January morning, I readied myself for a drive that would take me from my home in New Jersey to nearly across the state. The weather forecast was bleak; a wintry mix of sleet and ice would coat Interstate 95, making my solo ride west a bit dicey.

I grabbed my car keys and a small dog crate and headed for the front door. I dreaded the forty-minute trip, but I was excited too. Today, I would finally meet Teddy, an adorable Havanese mix that I was to foster.

Ever since I'd seen Teddy's photo on an adoption site, I had been smitten. In that photo, the little dog's chin rested lovingly on the tip of a man's large work boot. His face focused upward, presumably gazing with adoration at the object of his affection. But in the dog's eyes, I detected wistfulness.

As a writer and blogger about all things dog, I had developed an interest in fostering programs and wanted to experience the process firsthand to share my work more truthfully.

This would be an easy fostering experience, I reasoned. A dog like Teddy wouldn't remain in our care for long. Lynne, the head of the foster group with whom I was working, promised that Teddy would find his forever home long before a bond could possibly form between any of us. Applications from potential adopters were pouring in already. Who wouldn't want that sweet fuzzy face gazing up at them?

"I'll see you later," I called to my husband, Rich, as I headed out the front door. I didn't pause for a response. I did not have his blessing on this outing.

I tossed the crate into the back of the car and swung myself into the driver's seat. Lost in thought, I was startled when the car door wouldn't close. Someone was holding it open.

"Move over," Rich said. "I'm coming with you."

At first I didn't budge, refusing to surrender my position in the driver's seat.

"I thought you said you didn't want any part of this," I said.

"I don't. But you're picking up a strange dog, the weather is bad, and you might need help."

Help? Hadn't he seen that photo of this sweet angelic dog?

"C'mon. Hand over the keys," Rich persisted.

I did and slid over. He was right.

We drove in silence for a few minutes before he spoke again.

"Okay. Remind me again, *why* we are doing this?" he asked. "I have nothing against dogs, it's just that . . ." He searched for words. "It's just that this is too hard right now."

I got ready to come back at him with the standard-issue answer as to why people foster; that we were fostering our second dog because it was a meaningful way to help homeless dogs. It kept them out of shelters and provided a less stressful transfer experience that helped them adjust more easily to their new lives in permanent homes.

But he knew all this. The answer he sought went deeper than that. Out on the main road, the windshield wipers battled the sleet and rain. *Whoosh whoosh. Whoosh whoosh.* The rhythmic back and forth motion centered my thoughts.

Why was a fair question. Fostering could elicit strong emotional responses.

In light of recent life events, I'd come to have a better understanding of those people who, due to circumstances beyond their control, found their lives turned upside down. That, in essence, we didn't control our fates as much as I had once believed. Fostering, and the subsequent writing about it, was my way of dealing with that.

Everyone, at one time or another, seems to get "one of those years," and for us, the past six months had brought some sobering events. A health scare had found Rich hospitalized and visiting specialists for most of the summer. However, by Labor Day, we had rejoiced in the news that he was responding well to treatment and was on a path to healing.

But that happy news was quickly offset by the sudden death of our beloved eleven-year-old Portuguese water dog, Hooper. Typical of her breed, she was rambunctious, exuberant, intelligent, loyal, and clownish. Hoops, as we called her, was a daddy's girl. Rich had named her for a character from the movie *Jaws*, and she definitely drove the boat, and our household.

So caught up with the circumstances surrounding Rich's health, we missed small cues that she was ailing. She stumbled a bit, but she had always been a bit clumsy. We didn't know she had an illness that would take her quickly.

I stayed with Hooper during her final moments. I stroked her body and whispered in her ear, "When Dad is ready, please send him a new friend." For some reason, making that request brought me some comfort.

Anyone who has experienced the loss of a beloved pet knows that the grief experienced is not unlike the grief felt when a human family member or friend has passed. But more challenges were still to come.

In late October, the weather forecasters warned of an epic storm taking shape and aiming straight for our region. Talks that this storm would be unlike any experienced here before unnerved everyone. The meteorologists named it Hurricane Sandy.

As the news grew worse, our community reacted with a mix of dread and denial. Many who lived on the water heeded the forecasters' warnings and left, booking hotel rooms and crashing with friends and relatives inland. Those like us, residing on a slightly higher elevation, remained to bear witness to a monstrosity of nature none of us had ever witnessed before.

The night the storm made land, no one slept. The sounds of groans, cracks, and thumps played out against the unrelenting roar of the wind and pelting rain. Trees bent until they snapped, some falling to the ground with a sickening thud.

Within twenty-four hours, our community had gone from storm warning to storm mourning. Through cell phones and police patrols, stories reached us that the barrier island had been breached, causing waves to crest over the roofs of homes down island, resulting in massive widespread flooding. A major bridge had washed away, and sand dunes had overtaken major roadways. In our immediate vicinity, the homes of our neighbors had taken on several feet of water. Our home had been spared by a few minutes and a change of tide.

Finding their way back to storm-ravaged homes the next day, our neighbors began to comprehend just how much their lives had been changed. With their homes now uninhabitable, several came to stay with us, some arriving at our steps in a canoe. Distraught and numb, they sobbed as they surrendered their salvaged belongings contained in plastic shopping bags: jewelry, personal documents, photos.

Weeks went by as the great "Dry Out" proceeded. Our home became a base camp of sorts, and I assumed the role of laundress, linen changer, and keeper of the food and drink. The camaraderie of a weary band of neighbors meeting at the end of a long day was a bright spot. All we could do was offer them some comfort after hours spent scavenging whatever they could from their homes. Each day, the mountains of discarded furnishings, appliances, and personal items grew taller.

When our neighbors eventually found housing elsewhere, our home became empty and quiet. Despite the advent of the Christmas season, our nearly abandoned neighborhood was plunged into darkness; no house or holiday lights to lend cheer, no dinner gatherings with talk of storm news, no pitter-patter of dog paws or a furry chin resting on our laps.

In the evenings, I sought comfort in writing, and my interest in fostering grew stronger. At this unlikely time, I was ready to take on my first "client."

Our first foster, Ginger Snap, a rescue from Appalachia, came and went quickly. A frizzy little copper-toned terrier mix, she was so insecure that she'd fall asleep while standing on our staircase just inside the front door, ready for a fast escape. As much as she needed love and care, she had learned to run from humans. Happily, Ginger found a good home right in town.

And then I saw that picture of Teddy. For some reason, it spoke to me, and I put in a request to be his foster. Teddy's owner had fallen on hard times and could no longer keep him. I would later learn that by his current age of three, Teddy had already lost two homes.

"This is our exit," I said to Rich. We pulled off the highway into the parking lot of a store called Seasonal World, which was in the throes of post-holiday sales.

"Now what?" he asked.

"We wait."

"This dog sounds like a nice dog. Why would someone let him go?" Rich asked. I noticed that he had become emotionally engaged despite his initial resistance.

"I don't know," I answered. "Maybe his cuteness was a curse. Maybe he was purchased as a gift for Christmas, or a birthday, and then when the novelty wore off, he was no longer wanted."

"Who would do that?" Rich asked, frowning.

"Lots of people," I said. "You'd be surprised."

A gray car entered the parking lot. It slowed, and as it neared us, the woman driving made eye contact with me. She parked her car next to ours and smiled toward us. And then there he was in all his glory. Teddy appeared, perched on the woman's lap, like a curious meerkat, staring at us. He was a tussled mess but as adorable as his photo.

I realized that in the few photos I'd seen of Teddy, there hadn't been one of his backside. "I hope he doesn't have a white-tipped tail," I said. I had a weakness for dogs with white-tipped tails.

As if on cue, Teddy ran to the passenger side of the woman's car. With his back to us, he swished his full tail back and forth, displaying a flash of bright white that looked like he was waving a flag of surrender.

I should have accepted his offer on the spot, but the battle for his new home was not to be over so quickly.

"Well," Rich said, "go get him."

The nice lady from the foster group placed the scraggly dog in my arms, along with a bottle of pills for his Lyme disease treatment. She informed me that Teddy might have a bad tooth.

She also said he needed a professional grooming, which was an understatement. "He was filthy," she said. "The water was black after his first bath, and he was so matted he couldn't walk properly or wag his tail. We just kept cutting."

She kissed Teddy on his head. "He's so sweet," she said. "But I think he's a little depressed. He hasn't had it so easy."

In the car, Teddy sniffed us and his surroundings. The sky had cleared, and he soon fell asleep on my lap bathed in a patch of sun. I buried my nose in his soft fur and then took a good look at him.

His markings were beautiful, as if painted by an artist on a ceramic figurine. His face perfectly divided black and white with eyes the deep brown color of a chocolate bar. A dark gray wooly "sweater" covered his body, ending where his white legs stuck out. And of course there was that full tail with its white end.

In him I sensed a resigned, steady quality—calmly accepting yet another group of humans who were taking him someplace new.

Nearing home, Rich made a surprising detour and pulled into the parking lot of a store.

"What are you doing?" I asked.

"The dog looks hungry," he replied, getting out of the car. "I won't be long."

Teddy did not take his eyes off the store's entrance, waiting for Rich's return. When he came back to the car, Rich was holding a small white package of freshly ground meat. I knew Teddy had sensed an opportunity. Dogs are very good at spotting suckers.

In our home, Teddy settled in smoothly. He was no trouble at all and really didn't want to do much more than sleep. I set about doing my job as a foster parent. I kept an eye on Teddy's physical and emotional state while reading the applications of his prospective "parents." Many had been captivated by him.

"I'm going to take him to meet some of our neighbors," I told Rich a few days into Teddy's stay with us. "Maybe someone local might want to adopt him."

It worked. In one day, I had a taker. My neighbor, Maureen, who lived just across the street, fell in love with Teddy. She filled out all the required paperwork and gave me a check to cover Teddy's adoption fee.

There was one hitch, however. Maureen had not yet moved back into her storm-damaged home. "Can you hold on to Teddy for a week or so?" she asked. "My house needs a little more renovation."

Of course we didn't mind. Teddy was easy to have around. By now, however, I'd begun to notice a bond forming between this dog and Rich. In the evenings, Rich brushed Teddy, who then proceeded to curl up and nap on Rich's chest while we all watched TV.

I suggested that Maureen stop by to visit Teddy every few days. But this did not sit well with Teddy. Maybe he had come to associate visits from "strange" women with yet more trips to a strange house. Maybe he was ready to put a stop to it. On one occasion, when Maureen approached to hold him, Teddy jumped up on the sofa to hide behind Rich, peeking over Rich's shoulder, barking.

Does he have some behavior issues after all? I wondered.

"Come back in a few days," I advised my discouraged neighbor.

I called several female friends, asking them to come over to see how Teddy reacted to their arrival. Teddy greeted their visits with tail wags and kisses.

It appeared he somehow understood that Maureen wanted to take him away from a place he regarded as his new home.

"What do I do?" I asked Rich. "Are you sure you don't want to keep him?"

"No," Rich said, "you made a deal. He's going to his new home. He'll be fine."

But I wasn't buying it. I made the same inquiry each night. "Are you *sure*?"

The next evening while out for dinner, I relayed my predicament to a fellow dog lover, my friend Angie. She put down her drink and put her face close to mine. "You *must* keep him," she said.

I told her how all of this had confused me. "I feel like a foster failure, a fraud, a fake."

"No," she said. "You're only human. That dog needs you and Rich, and you both need him."

I *had* witnessed how Rich talked so sweetly to Teddy each night, and how happy Rich had become. This little dog had filled our home with a lightness we hadn't experienced for some time. The words I had whispered to Hooper came back to me. *Didn't I ask her to send Dad a new friend?*

Still we held fast. But on the night Maureen arrived to take Teddy to her home, she was greeted by yet another Teddy tantrum.

Maureen sat down and sighed. "I don't think this going to work," she said. "It's apparent that he wants you to keep him, and I don't want a dog that doesn't want me."

The room grew dead silent. I looked at Rich then, asked him pointedly, "What do you want to do?"

Rich sat, the palms of his hands pressed hard against his eyes. He let out a sigh and looked at Teddy, who was intently studying Rich's face.

"Tear up her check," Rich finally answered. He got up, threw on a coat, and disappeared out the door, escaping into the cover of darkness from the emotions of the moment.

I looked at Teddy, then at Maureen, searching for the right words.

"You know this is not what I had planned," I said.

"I know," Maureen said. She managed a tearful smile at Teddy. "Sometimes *we* don't get to choose."

She left me alone with Teddy. He seemed all right with the situation, trotting about, happily wagging his white flag-like tail.

"Come here," I called to him. He jumped up on my lap and kissed my nose.

I reached for a white tissue, and before I touched it to my eyes, I waved it at him.

"We surrender too," I whispered in his ear. "Welcome home."

Rusty to the Rescue

Audrey Leach

The first time I met Rusty Dog he was curled up in the back seat of the car. He was a beautiful deep red with feathering in his tail and a ruff with tips of gold. His right leg was shaved from his hip on down, and his eyes were a deep soulful brown. Rusty Dog was a mixed collie and chow chow with the nose and ears of the collie and the dignity and intelligence of the chow chow. He lifted and cocked his head and gazed into my eyes. He decided to let me get in the car.

The next thing I knew, Rusty Dog climbed through the opening from the back seat to the front seat. He sat on my lap, gave me a nuzzle, and proceeded to the floor to lie on my feet. This was no small feat for a dog who had been shot in the hip. The shattered socket had been replaced with a ball so he could stand, leaving his right leg two inches shorter than his other legs.

I met Rusty because I was going on a date with his human, Chris. I do not really know what made me go on that first date. I had not dated for over two years, and that was fine with me, as I was content being single. Marriage did not seem to be in my future. Then out of the blue, I got a phone call from this friend of my brother-in-law, asking me out. I had met the man four years ago and gone out with him once. We did not have one thing in common, so we went our separate ways—until I got that phone call.

My date showed up that Saturday night with Rusty Dog (Nail was his middle name) in the car. He had rescued Rusty from the middle of a remote dirt road. Someone had shot him clean through his leg at the hip. Chris stopped, took him home, and then to the vet, who sent them to Michigan State University. Their vet school doctors performed the surgery for the hip socket replacement.

Chris had just divorced and was devastated. But having Rusty gave him someone to care for when he had nothing else. As for me, I thought there was no one I could connect to, no one I could find common ground with to build a relationship or future with, until that date with Chris. And Rusty Dog.

We went to the movies. Rusty Dog went with us. He went to the park with us, the grocery store, meetings with friends—every time I got into the car, Rusty would climb through from the back to the front. He would reverse the process every time I got out.

That September we hunted for mushrooms, and Rusty came along with us to a beautiful wooded hillside and open fields. This piece of land would later become the site for our first home. We went swimming one day at the end of the summer, and of course Rusty Dog jumped in right along with us. Lying in the sun afterwards, Chris took my hand. He told me Rusty taught him how to trust again, to love again. "Watching how you care about Rusty, how you treat him, shows me the kind of person you are," Chris said. "A person with a good heart."

I was at a loss for words. I thought I'd found a wonderful friend with the bonus of a wonderful dog. Chris's words took me by surprise but also touched my heart. I discovered I loved the man—and his dog. Chris was giving me dreams I didn't even know I had. I decided that any man who would rescue a dog and drive him to the university for a costly surgery was the kind of man you could count on. He and Rusty Dog had won me over. I opened my heart to both of them.

On our wedding day, Rusty Dog waited in the car for us.

We bought the land where we had hunted for mushrooms and began to build our house. One day while we were up on the roof, it was clear that Rusty could not stand to be on the ground. "Come on, Rusty, you can do it, come on . . ." And that dog climbed up an eight-foot ladder one rung at a time until he reached us on the roof. Rusty Nail would not be left out of any situation. It was almost as if he wanted to prove that even though his hip limited him, he would do anything for us. I believe he never forgot that he was rescued after having been shot and left to die on that dirt road.

Rusty Dog had a huge heart. He was loyal and loving and gave his all. He thought he was a lap dog even though he was almost two feet tall and weighed forty pounds. He would climb on my lap, take my hand in his two front paws, and let out the biggest sigh. Then he would take a little nap right there in my lap. He limped when he walked but somehow figured out how to jump straight up in tall grass, pushing off with his good leg to bound through the field like a rabbit. He was the best guard dog and alerted us to anyone or anything that trespassed on his territory. I felt safe with him around. I always felt like Rusty Nail had my back.

The day came when a baby crib arrived. Rusty Dog knew something was up. He would look at me, then look at the crib. He stopped sleeping on my lap even though I coaxed him to come up. Instead, he would lie on my feet with a worried look. We still took Rusty with us everywhere we went and gave him special treats. I was worried about how he would respond to a baby.

The day we brought our daughter home from the hospital, I placed her in the crib. Rusty sat next to her and watched her for about a half an hour, then went to the front door to be let out. I did not see Rusty for three days. I was so worried by the second day that I was in tears. I called him and searched where I could, but with a newborn, I had little time to spare. On the third day of his absence, Rusty came home at his regular feeding time.

I cried again as he crawled up on my lap. He sat on his haunches, placed his face next to mine, and nuzzled. I told him I was so relieved he was home and to never do that again. He made some whimpering sounds and nuzzled some more. Then he got down from my lap and went straight under the crib. There he spent most of his time every day and every night until our daughter outgrew that crib. Then he took over the job of watching her.

Rusty Dog would let that child roll and crawl all over him. When she learned to walk, she would grab hold of the hair on the back of the dog's neck. Then he would slowly walk with her hanging on until she no longer needed to hold on.

As she turned into a toddler who could talk, she'd say, "Come on, Rusty Dawg," and he would be there. If he thought she was toddling in the wrong direction, he would nudge her in the opposite direction.

We had our Rusty Dog until he was probably around thirteen, and then cancer took him. We buried him on the land where he lived with us. I like to think he is jumping around in that tall grass, chasing those rabbits, ears alert, the sunshine pouring on his beautiful rusty-red coat. Watching over his property.

Rusty Dog brought us together as a family. Yes, he was rescued, but he did a lot of rescuing himself—rescuing his human from a broken heart, being a loving companion, showing us we could trust again. By being a watchful guard dog and a loving protector of our family, Rusty Nail Dog rescued us all.

An Angel Came Calling

Chrissy Drew

We picked her up from the cargo hangar at the airport. It took all but two seconds and we were mush.

There she was, all four pounds and nine inches. A white furball of cuteness, sheltered in a huge doggie carrier. Big brown eyes staring out the slits of the metal carrier. Tail wagging causing her whole miniature body to shake. It was as if she'd known us forever and we were being reunited. But we weren't—it was our first introduction to her.

My eighty-seven-year-old next-door neighbor had recently passed away. His daughter, Ruthel, was his caregiver and lived with him. He was an active senior. He walked nearly every day. He'd pick up pebbles at the nearby track, and each time he completed a lap, he'd put a pebble in his pocket to remember how many times he went around. Brilliant, right? He would also come and sit with my husband and me when we were outside and tell so many stories.

As it goes, he was getting too old to drive. I've often found that when the elderly lose their ability to drive, they feel they have lost their independence. My neighbor's eyesight was getting worse, and he started falling periodically.

Early one morning, I noticed an ambulance next door. I went out to investigate. Ruthel saw me and said her father had fallen in the bathroom and appeared to have broken some ribs. I walked up to the ambulance to let him know I'd be praying for him. As he so often did, he smiled and gave me a thumbs-up. Off to the hospital he went, and he never returned home. He was sent to a nursing facility, where my husband and I visited him. I made him laugh—one last time.

His death was a huge blow to his children. Soon the house became big and lonely for Ruthel, and she began searching for something to fill the void—something or someone to nurture and love. She decided to get a puppy. Her dad had preferred they not have animals, but now she had the option.

She wanted a special puppy, a shih tzu. There were no local breeders, and after doing some internet searching, she came across a breeder of shih tzus located in Missouri. Getting the puppy from there to here in California was going to be a challenge for Ruthel. It would not be cheap. But she was determined. It was love at first sight with a puppy named Isabella.

With all the vetting on both sides and paperwork to fill out, it would be a couple of weeks before Ruthel would have her puppy. The wait was almost unbearable for her.

I had no idea she was planning this until I got a call from her asking if I could take her to the airport to pick up her puppy.

What? A puppy?

I knew caring for a puppy would be a huge responsibility for a person who had never owned one before. But in my heart and soul, I knew this would be a good thing for her, so of course I said yes.

She continued her correspondence with the breeder, making sure she would have everything she needed once Isabella arrived. There were potty-training mats to purchase and toys and beds and food. Ruthel was diligent about reading and learning everything she needed to know before the puppy arrived to make the transition a smooth one—for both of them. I was impressed. I scheduled an appointment with the airline to pick up the puppy, and Ruthel and I arrived in plenty of time.

At last, the transfer paperwork was completed. Those waiting in the cargo area oohed and ahhed over the puppy. She was already the center of attention. Ruthel wasn't having any of that. She grabbed the carrier and rushed out the door with me on her heels.

It seemed as though the car was parked miles away—the anticipation of taking the puppy out of the carrier and holding her was almost more than we could bear. The puppy seemed content, and she didn't even bark. It was like she knew she was home.

As soon as we got the carrier to the car, Ruthel gently retrieved the puppy. I, of course, had to hold this ball of happiness. Aunty Chrissy had rights, you know.

Ruthel had already chosen a new name: Angel. She felt the name was appropriate, as this little darling was a blessing from God. Angel sat and squirmed on Ruthel's lap on the way home from the airport. The puppy was a bundle of energy as she licked and kissed her new mommy.

And having that puppy was like having a new baby. It wasn't long before Angel got used to her new home. Ruthel brought her over to me so I could see her and hold her. It was my reward for taking her to the airport. Visitation rights.

Angel provides a much-needed, two-way unconditional rescued love. Ruthel finally has that special something to care for, and Angel is right at home. It was a match made in heaven.

As for me, I have the best of both worlds. I get to hold that ball of cuteness for as long as I wish—and then hand back the responsibility Ruthel has so wonderfully met with all her heart.

The Shepherd's Instincts

Wanda Dyson

My husband, Jim, and I took in a great many dogs during our years of doing canine rescue. We had Dobermans and rottweilers, setters and terriers, little dogs and big dogs, nice dogs and nasty ones. One of the few breeds that managed to elude us was the German shepherd. I'm not sure why, but it was almost twenty-five years before Whitney came to us.

Whitney was a solid black, long-haired German shepherd with a fear problem. She was afraid of everything. When we took her for a walk, she stayed behind us. When she was with the pack, she was in the corner or out of the way. In the kennel, she curled up in a tight ball as far from everyone as possible. People, dogs, horses, Frisbees, loud noises, gunshots, thunder, the washing machine, the dishwasher. She was afraid of it all.

And one of her greatest fears? Chickens. She was terrified of them. If we took her anywhere near the coop, she'd cower at our feet, howling as though all forty of our chickens were swarming all over her, spurring and pecking with unrelenting fervor.

116

One of the problems with canine rescue is that you don't always receive a background on the animal. Was Whitney attacked by a rooster as a puppy? There was no way of knowing, but she had so many fears that it really didn't matter in the long run.

Whitney had been with us for about a month when she woke me up in the middle of the night, barking as if a burglar were trying to steal her kibble. I climbed out of bed and looked out the bedroom window.

"Jim! Wake up!" I grabbed my jeans off the chair and started climbing into them. When we'd gone to bed at ten, it was barely snowing, and no weather report had mentioned any real accumulation. It was now three in the morning, and the snow looked to be more than a foot deep.

"What's the matter?"

"We're in the middle of a blizzard, and it just collapsed the chicken coop." All I could think of were all those chickens trapped under wood and snow, trying to find a way out. I could only hope we'd get there in time.

Now, once upon a time, something like this would have resulted in Jim's telling me to go back to bed while he went out and dealt with it, but those days were gone. Neither of us knew why at the time, but he was having difficulty doing almost anything anymore. When our car broke down around midnight about a mile from home, I was the one who walked home to get the other car while Jim stayed with our young daughter, Jayme. That never would have happened just a few years earlier. Jim always took pride in taking care of his "girls."

But now, he could barely make it down the stairs. How in the world was he going to be able to struggle through snow this deep all the way down to the chicken coop?

Downstairs, Whitney was still barking, so before suiting up, I stuck my head in the indoor portion of the kennel. "We're up, Whitney. You can stop barking now."

She continued to bark and pace, so I opened her cage and let her out. She ran into the house and then down the hall to the back door.

The barking stopped, but she continued to pace. "I'm glad you're anxious to go out in that storm," I said to her while I laced up my boots. "But it's not just snowing, it's a whiteout. You're gonna take two steps out there and come running back inside."

Jim finally joined me and grabbed his gloves. "Why is she out?"

"She was in there having a hissy fit, so I let her out."

"Well, once she sees what we're about to go out in, she'll change her mind."

"That's what I told her."

Bracing ourselves for the onslaught, I opened the back door and headed out. A black streak passed me and started plowing through the snow in the direction of the chicken coop. I looked over at Jim, but he had his head down. I tugged his sleeve. "Did you see that?"

"See what?"

"Whitney! She's going ahead of us, clearing a path for us to walk in!"

"Remind me to give her an extra treat."

Jim continued to struggle, so Whitney and I made it down to the coop long before he did. Half the building was flattened while the other half was struggling to stay upright.

Whitney started digging near one of the doors, and I could hear the hens inside, squawking loudly in protest of their home collapsing. By the time Jim made it to the coop, Whitney and I had just about cleared the doorway.

Now my concern was for my husband. He wasn't breathing right. In fact, he was struggling to breathe at all. "Are you okay?"

"I'm fine. I promise. Just a little short of breath. Can you get that door open?"

"I think so." I had to pull a couple of times, but I did get the door halfway open. Jim eased past me, and a few minutes later,

118

he stuck his head back out. "It looks like they're all okay. If we lost any, it's only one or two, but I don't think so. I'm just going to brace this corner and it should hold until morning."

"Should we clear the top?"

"Absolutely."

I was barely aware of Whitney's continued digging efforts as I cleaned the snow from the top of the coop to keep the weight from forcing it down. Then she barked at me. I stopped brushing at snow and looked over at her. "What's your problem?"

She barked again and went back to digging in the collapsed portion of the coop. Setting the broom aside, I went over and knelt down beside her. "What is it?"

She looked at me and tilted her head as if to say, "Can't you hear it?"

And then I did.

"Jim, one of the birds is trapped over here!"

Once Jim joined me, we were able to brush away snow and lift the corner of the coop high enough for Whitney to stick her head inside and pull the hen out.

"Well, would you look at that?" I took the bird from Whitney's mouth, amazed that she'd gone after it, and more amazed that she hadn't killed it.

I put the bird in the still-standing portion of the coop and cleared the small ramp so that they could go into the run if they felt so inclined.

Jim and I started back up to the house, but Whitney started running toward the barn, barking at us as she went. Jim turned and followed after her, so I did as well.

I saw it before Jim did. One end of the run-in attached to the barn was bowing under the weight of the snow. We had several horses inside that run-in, and a collapse would seriously injure if not kill some of them.

"I'll get another broom out of the garage," Jim yelled to me.

The wind was blowing sideways, and the sting of the snow on our faces was nothing short of painful. But when you know you have animals in trouble, you do what you have to do. Watching Whitney run around saving animals that she was so afraid of was nothing short of amazing.

We cleared the barn roof, and it held up through the rest of the storm. No animal lives were lost. I credit Whitney for that fact. She knew animals were in trouble, and she was willing to overcome her fears to be the shepherd she was born to be.

But it was more than the storm and the animals. After clearing the barn, we headed back to the house. Whitney stayed right in front of us, plowing a path for us.

Back inside, she refused to go back into the kennel. Jim and I let her be and went into the kitchen to put on some coffee and warm up. Whitney put her head on Jim's thigh and kept it there, nudging him from time to time.

Neither of us understood what she was doing or why. She wasn't one to cuddle or to seek attention or affection, so this was new behavior for her. But Jim was more than happy to sit there, drink his coffee, and pet Whitney.

When Jim went out the next day to plow, Whitney went with him. When he came in, she was still with him. And she stayed with him until I was putting dinner on the table and Jim told me he couldn't breathe.

The doctor said he was in congestive heart failure. In spite of being airlifted to Johns Hopkins for emergency surgery, Jim didn't make it. And when I arrived home from the hospital, Whitney was howling in a way that I can only describe as keening.

To calm her down, I tossed one of Jim's dirty T-shirts into her kennel, and she curled up on top of it and calmed down. I couldn't blame her. I wanted to curl up on one of his shirts too, but I had a daughter who was grieving the loss of her beloved daddy. My life would need to focus on her for a while.

I made a few calls, explained that Jim had passed, and made arrangements for the dogs to go to other foster homes. It was going to be weeks before they would all go, and I would hate to see the empty kennels, but I knew that my daughter was going to need me more than the dogs would.

But one dog wasn't waiting around to go to another foster home.

A few days later, when I returned from the funeral home, I found Whitney had passed away in her kennel. She was lying on Jim's shirt.

> "I have found that when you are deeply troubled, there are things you get from the silent devoted companionship of a dog that you can get from no other source."
>
> —Doris Day

The Bonus Dog

Delores E. Topliff

"Mom, when can we get a dog?"

My two young sons had been asking this question more frequently lately. But conditions weren't right yet. They needed to be older than ages six and eight to train and take care of a pet. We would also need to save extra funds to buy food and pay for possible vet visits. Most of all, I wanted to wait until we had a place of our own with a fenced yard—not sharing a rental house in a Dallas suburb with a fellow young single mom also raising two little boys.

"We will get one," I promised my sons each time with a smile, sure I was telling the truth. "But it's important to wait until we can do it right. It needs to be an outside dog for the times you're at school and I'm at work. But you can start thinking about what kind of dog you want. Let's discuss ideas, say your prayers, and we'll see what happens." I figured we had plenty of time to navigate the process to choose our first dog, and do it right. We'd follow a wise sequence of steps and be happy with the results.

My sons must have really said their prayers, because God surprised us sooner than anyone expected.

Before we could move into a place of our own, I had to replace our worn-out, high-mileage Volkswagen Squareback. It had served our family well for years but had reached that point where expensive repairs were happening more and more often—alternator, timing belt, fuel pump . . . It made more sense to replace the car than spend more money fixing an aging vehicle.

Besides, every time it rained, water from puddles splashed through holes we could not find in the car's back floorboard until we had one to two inches of water. My boys were in no danger, and it didn't hurt them, except they had to hold their feet up to keep from getting wet. We laughed each time, but the more it occurred, the less funny it got.

I worked overtime, saving up money to pay cash for a car. I started investigating various makes and models. My father sold cars at his used car lot two thousand miles away, so he gave me tips on things to look for and problems to avoid. Although he ran a used car lot himself, he suggested I not go to a lot but instead check the "For Sale by Owner" classified ads.

My sons suggested ideas—year, model, size, color—and we all knew it had to be a good price. It should be as new as we could afford without going into debt. It had to get good gas mileage, and with two boys in the family, it could *not* look like an old lady's car. That eliminated quite a few options right there.

We studied pictures and discussed domestic or foreign make, stick shift versus automatic (I'm sure they hoped to drive it in a few years), front wheel or rear wheel drive, and more. They loved Jeeps, but those used too much fuel. Cute little sports cars were eliminated in spite of usually good gas mileage, since insurance and repair costs ran high. Our list for what we could not buy was growing longer than our list of possible choices.

Then one Friday after work I read a "For Sale by Owner" ad offering a two-year-old Ford Galaxie in great condition at a sacrifice price because the owners had to move by the end of the month. It sounded good, so the nice mom we shared a house with and I arranged a play date for all four boys so she could drive me to see the car in case I bought it on the spot. We made an appointment and drove thirty miles to a pleasant neighborhood to take a look.

They were a sweet young couple who had sold their home to live in an RV for a few years. Their almost-new Ford Galaxie was blue with fancy chrome, very clean, had low mileage, a great service history, and a discounted price for cash payment. After my test drive, they agreed to transfer the title so I could drive it home that very day.

"Do you have children?" the wife asked.

"Two little boys," I answered.

"We don't yet, but we're looking forward to it," she said. She was cradling an adorable white miniature toy poodle in her arms. "Do your boys like dogs?"

"Actually, they do. They talk about getting one, but we're not ready yet."

Both of their faces broke out in smiles. The husband said, "We wonder if maybe you might be ready, because our car comes with a surprise bonus. Meet Lacy Brooke."

He petted her soft curly fur. "We know it's not fair to take her traveling with us—she'd be miserable. So we prayed that whoever bought our Galaxie would have a family and want her. She plays great with children, is completely housebroken, and her shots are up to date. We're also including plenty of toys and a collar." He pointed to two bags near their front door. "We have everything you need. What do you think?"

What did I think? She wasn't at all what our family had in mind, but she was the cutest thing I'd ever seen. She looked more like an adorable stuffed toy than a dog all four boys at home could rough and tumble with. And yet, she was gentle and sweet. She would probably cultivate more of those same qualities in them as they cared for her. I reached out to pet her, and her perfect raspy pink tongue licked my fingers.

"She likes you," the wife said. "We have extra bags of dog food and treats too."

It was a good thing our housemate, Judy, was with me. I turned to her. "What do *you* think?"

She laughed. "I think she's pretty darling. How can you resist? I think we can work it out."

One look in Lacy Brooke's trusting baby blue eyes (that exactly matched the car's blue color), and I was sold. Even her playful bark was cute. It was almost like she chose us, and the car was our lesser bonus prize.

We signed papers and drove back home in two cars. "Come see what I bought," I called to all four boys as they tumbled outside. First they walked around the outside of the Galaxie, and then I opened the door to show them our surprise. "Meet Lacy Brooke," I said and held her in my arms so they could see and pet her. "She comes with the car." I'll bet all our neighbors heard their excited shouts.

Lacy Brooke didn't seem to have any trouble adjusting to our home. Nor did all four boys have trouble adjusting to her. It was like she'd been with us always, and we were meant to be together. I believe that animals know when they're loved, and she certainly was. Her affectionate licks and short wagging tail certainly made the boys feel loved too.

Aaron, my younger son, had been thin far too long from frequent sicknesses like recurring strep throat and tonsillitis, until we finally had his tonsils and adenoids out. Even after that, his recovery was slow and uphill—until Lacy Brooke came. Then, as Aaron thought about what was important for her to eat, and when, he did better at feeding himself. They both flourished. It turned out that what our household of four young boys needed all along was an adorable white miniature toy poodle who rewarded their constant attention with endless love.

As the years passed, all four boys grew tall and strong. I was offered a job teaching and being principal in a school on a ranch in the Rocky Mountain foothills of the Pacific Northwest. We visited and loved the place. Although I would drive the Galaxie north, towing a trailer, all three of us knew it wouldn't be the right setting for Lacy Brooke. Because they loved her, my boys realized she'd be better off staying with our close friends in the household we were leaving behind. We took plenty of pictures that we still have, and we gave her hugs and treats.

Both sons were bigger and stronger by the time we moved northwest to our very different life. For after-school chores, my older son, Andrew, signed up to learn skills and help at the farm's small sawmill. My now much healthier younger son, Aaron, first cared for horses and mastered driving a four- and then a six-horse hitch team.

Soon after that, he trained to manage a flock of 103 Romney sheep. He helped with birthing lambs and shearing wool. This involved running up and down pasture hills and valleys with our second dog, a blue heeler, to shepherd the sheep. My son's experiences day in and day out, caring for the flock with the blue heeler, eventually led to his becoming a successful doctor.

That's a different story, but our family knows it all began when we needed a newer car. And along with our Ford Galaxie came a bonus prize—our sweet white miniature toy poodle, Lacy Brooke.

Going Home with Mithril

Claudia Wolfe St. Clair

The time has come to downsize from my dream house in the Old West End in Toledo. After many years in this historic district, I'm returning to the family home on Lake Erie with my dog, Mithril.

Tolkien fans may recognize the subtle reference to dwarves' silver, which is where Mithril got her name. She started her life with us as a favor to a friend. We were asked to puppy-sit for two weeks. At the time, I was pregnant, far from family and friends, and feeling very lonely. My husband was serving at Fort Bragg, North Carolina, back then and was away a great deal of the time. Having a furry presence that required attention and frequent walks was a huge comfort for me. The secret pact with Mithril's owner was pure subterfuge: if I fell in love with the dog, I could keep her. Of course I did!

Mithril required an outdoor visit every two hours to empty her tiny bladder. This broke me in to the needs of my future baby. I would be sleepless for a long time to come. I adjusted to Mithril's routine. There's nothing like puppy love. And the puppy continued to grow at an alarming rate.

Mithril's mother was a small terrier mix, which we expected our pup to become. Four weeks into this adventure, she was twice the size of her mother and littermates. Two months later it was apparent that the puppy-daddy was likely a sheepdog. Mithril's black markings on her white coat made her the classic shaggy dog. She was all boundless energy and enthusiasm.

My due date came and went. My whole family arrived for the birth—my parents, brother, and grandfather. Another week went by, and my dad, brother, and grandfather had to leave, but Mom stayed. Another day turned into another week, and I was now two weeks overdue, beyond tired, and weary of waiting. Mom took over Mithril's care, but Mithril kept her eyes on me. She knew something was going on.

Mithril was six months old and ready to be spayed. I scheduled her procedure with our vet, who happened to be President Jimmy Carter's brother-in-law. But my water broke in the wee hours the same day Mithril was scheduled at the vet's. My husband was away on a field exercise, so it was up to my mom to attend to her daughter and her grand-puppy that day in September.

Before leaving for the hospital, Mom took a photo of Mithril and me beside the empty and waiting crib. Hospital first, vet second for Mom. My husband was called in from the field and made it in time to greet our son, Ian. Then he returned to the field.

When Ian and I came home, Mithril somehow seemed to think this new caterwauling creature was all hers. She rocked the cradle with her nose. If a little hand slipped out, she would gently push it back into the cradle.

Once Ian was crawling, he thought nothing of taking the bone Mithril was chewing right out of her mouth. And she let him. She'd patiently wait until he dropped it and then take it back. Ian noted the bone was something to chew on, so he did the same. This bone sharing could go on, back and forth, all afternoon.

As happens in the military, orders came down for a change of duty station. We would be moving to the Republic of Panama in the new year. During the packing of our household goods, we heard Mithril cry out. She'd never made a sound like that before. We ran to her and found that Ian had pulled himself up to a standing position by hanging on to her facial hair. He was weaving all over, not falling, with Mithril in pain. The look in her eyes said "Save me!" She simply would not harm Ian to extricate herself from his grip. We loosened his fingers one by one and praised Mithril for being a good girl.

My parents came to take Mithril during the move. Unbeknownst to me, my husband had offered Mithril to my dad . . . to keep. Dad gave him the only advice he was ever to give my husband: "This is Claudia's dog. Mithril is not yours to give away. If I were you, I wouldn't put her in a position to choose between you and the dog. She might just choose the dog."

We received word that quarters would not be available for months. Rather than accepting temporary lodgings in a strange place with neither transportation nor familiar faces, we opted for my husband to go ahead. Ian and I would join Mithril at my parents' house on the lake in Ohio.

By the time we arrived in Ohio, Mithril was following my dad everywhere. She sat beside his chair watching the ships go by. She kept the yard free of squirrels, muskrats, and birds. We had an idyllic summer by the lake. We played. We fished. We waited. And waited. At last my husband sent for us, and our little family was reunited.

But an outbreak of parvovirus had struck Panama, so Mithril would have to wait a little longer to join us. Dogs were dying. We didn't want to put her at risk, so we left her in my parents' care.

Our hilltop quarters were on Fort Davis on the Atlantic side with the Panama Canal about five hundred yards away. In the back was the jungle. It was a small post. Ian and I took twice daily walks.

On our first walk, we found a dead bug that was twelve inches long without its head. I was horrified! How much larger would it have been with its head? Even worse . . . what ate its head? That was the first time I became acutely aware of the food chain. We might be at the top of it. We might be in the middle!

We were able to send for Mithril after the virus had run its course. She flew from Detroit to Miami. From Miami she flew to Panama City on the Pacific side. The distance between the Pacific and Atlantic was only fifty-two miles, so it was a short ride home. Well . . . home by way of the army kennel. Mithril was required to spend thirty days in quarantine. We visited her every day to exercise her. Ian was walking by then, and they made quite a pair.

I can't overstate the difficulty of keeping a toddler safe in the tropics. One never just stepped out the door without checking for snakes or some jungle creature. This is when Mithril's role took on greater proportions. She was more than my companion. She was our protector.

There were coatis, panthers, snakes, and lizards, some poisonous, some not, as well as poisonous frogs and insects, bats, and vultures. Mithril barked at everything that moved, and she kept the yard free of all creatures great and small. Thanks to her, we were able to spend most of our days playing outdoors in complete safety.

Before long another baby came along . . . a beautiful little girl, Gillian. Mithril was an old hand at this baby thing by then. She was an attentive, protective presence as Gillian grew to toddlerhood.

Orders came again for my husband to take a school assignment. We decided to spend the summer back in Ohio for the duration of that phase, freeing my husband to focus on his studies. We left Panama with two weeks notice, and Mithril was put on another flight back to Ohio.

It was another wonderful summer on Lake Erie. Mithril was happier away from the tropics. My parents enjoyed our company.

In the fall, our family was reunited at Fort Benning, Georgia. We were living post again. We fenced the backyard on Rainbow Avenue to contain Mithril and the children, and we enjoyed three years there.

With another baby on the way, we were ordered to Fort Myer, Virginia. We bought a home outside the Beltway, and Mithril had a new yard. But by the time Colin was born at Walter Reed, Mithril was not so interested in tending another baby. She let me be the mom for a change. She liked him much better when he was old enough to be attentive to her.

All three children loved Mithril to pieces. But she was always closest to me. Our relationship became a duo when the children were all in school, much like when she was a puppy. My husband was still away a great deal. But Mithril was by my side . . . always.

As children in the military, my kids had childhoods quite different from the one I had growing up. I had lived in one town with the continuity of many generations intermingling. Not so my children. Two factors provided some semblance of continuity for them. Summers spent with my parents at the lake offered the one stable location they could count on. The other factor was growing up with a beloved family pet, Mithril.

Years passed. The children have grown and gone, each living in a different state. They have families and cats and dogs of their own. All of the people who comprised my life are gone in one way or another. I am alone again.

The house on the lake is waiting for my return. Mithril's ashes have moved with me many times. I just couldn't bury her in a place where she hadn't lived. Now I can take her home. Really home.

The spot in the yard where she sat beside my dad is where she belongs. I'm going home with Mithril at last.

Rescue Garden

Michelle Janene

Apurebred two-year-old black cocker spaniel with the name of a white flower was the first.

I adopted Daisy Honey Bear from a vet whose customer could no longer care for her. Daisy and I moved out of my parents' home together and started the "adult" life. She soon earned a second middle name, Houdini, as she escaped everywhere I tried to corral her when I went to work. When she escaped before I got out the door, I laughed and gave her full run of the house.

I may have rescued Daisy from the vet, but her antics, exuberant play, and comforting snuggles saved me from loneliness and the crushing quiet of living on my own. She loved to play ball and chased after just about anything, which led to an injury from which she could not recover.

The next flower in my garden was Jaszmine, a white and black chiweenie. My goodness, how that girl loved to play. She relocated to a new city with me, comforting me through job losses, heartbreaks, and solitary nights. She lost her hearing after twelve years, but we found other ways to communicate. Never wanting to be too far from me, she'd sleep in the chair behind me at my desk for hours as I struggled to learn the craft of writing. At the end when she lost her sight too, she only wanted to stay beside me. Seventeen years together wasn't enough.

The quiet overwhelmed me, and the emptiness pulled me into a pit. After so many years with my faithful companion, I knew I'd never find another like her. But I couldn't be alone either. I needed to be rescued again, so I decided to find another four-legged baby.

I found a shelter that liberated small dogs from high-kill facilities. The barn-style building that housed the squirming, yapping, wagging bundles of joy was a cacophony of noise. This time I wanted two, in hopes they'd keep each other company while I was away.

I wound slowly between the playpens scattered around the floor. Wagging tails and yelps greeted me. How could I choose between all these adorable faces? Maybe two wasn't enough.

A movement caught my eye. She was climbing right up the side of her playpen. Another Houdini? I picked up the tricolored chiweenie before she flipped over the top and landed on her nose. She continued to scramble up on my shoulder and snuggled into my neck. "You picking me, girl? Or am I picking you?"

I set her down, then picked out another wiggling fur ball to see how they got along. The dog I was sure had chosen me and would be coming home soon was a little prankster. She darted from me, nipped the potential rival on the leg, and dashed back to stand boldly between my feet. This was repeated with a variety of other choices. "All right, are you coming to me to be saved if that dog retaliates, or are you warning off any others and claiming me for yourself?"

Poppy was the only puppy I brought home that day, and she quickly lived up to her name. Spring loaded, she had more explosive leaps than a bag of microwave popcorn. Her four-inch legs could launch her near to my waist and easily up on my pillow-top mattress. She wasn't much for playing ball, but she loved to disembowel her toys and kill the squeakers.

But most importantly, she filled the hole left by Jaszmine. She comforted me, driving out the loneliness, and she loved to snuggle. To this day, Poppy never lets me forget a mealtime—even if she has to start reminding me at 9:00 a.m. that it will be dinnertime at about 4:00 p.m.

But she was alone during the day while I taught. She needed a friend too.

I visited the SPCA around the corner a couple times a month, alternating with visits to the county pound near work. I even ventured across town to the city pound a few times. But a year passed and then another with no playmate for Poppy. I didn't want another puppy to have to train; housebreaking Poppy had been a challenge.

I wanted to find the right dog, one who needed a home as much as Poppy and I needed another friend. Three fur babies had rescued me. Now Poppy and I needed someone new to liberate—and to join the party. Then word came that the county pound was overcrowded and having a sale. Time to go look again.

At the pound, several rooms with pretty glass walls, toys, cots, and colorful blankets each held a few dogs on display. One little Chihuahua who looked like a fox was all alone.

"I'd like to see that one."

I was taken to a small room behind her display window, the door was opened between us, and we were left alone. I knelt on the floor and coaxed.

She inched toward me, low to the ground, tail tucked so tight it rubbed her belly. It took her almost five minutes to work her way the few feet to where I sat. I talked softly, encouraging her. She crawled onto my leg and stared at me with black eyes that betrayed her fear.

"So you want to come home with me?"

She trembled and stared. I petted her gently. She cringed, then crawled farther into my lap.

"I'll take that as a yes, little girl."

I filled out the paperwork, but I had to leave her there for a couple of days so they could spay her.

When I excitedly returned home, Poppy, now two years old, inspected me and the foreign scent. I tried to explain how the little brown Chihuahua who looked like a fox would be a good fit. Poppy tipped her head, not convinced.

I worried in the first few days after I brought one-year-old Ivy home. She came with some baggage. She ran from me, tail tucked, and hid behind furniture. If I sat still, she might eventually come to me. Even then, though, she cringed and shook. Her reactions spoke of abuse.

After a couple days of indifference, Poppy wanted to play. It took over a week before Ivy would join in. She would run and hide when I laughed at their antics, but maybe we would work out after all.

Slowly, Ivy started to recover from her past.

Today her tail wags. She now explodes with excitement when I return home. The fear is replaced with a jump-dance accompanied by a half-howl/half-talk to greet me.

Ivy's been with us three years, and now she seldom startles at feet moving toward her. Stomping feet or a slow, stalking march get her excited and ready to play. She goes down on her front knees, her rump in the air—her playtime stance. She bursts out of bed in the morning, leaping around, happy, nipping at fingers, bounding around the house, as Poppy and I struggle to get our eyes open and our feet moving.

My four-legged rescue garden reminds me every day to love with my whole heart, unbound and wild; to forget past hurts and instead play; that life is better with others. And that we all need to be rescued from something.

Leap of Faith

Sarah Parshall Perry

She only lies on our bed.

(There she is now. She is flicking one of her large brown eyes at me as I write. Her tail is tucked up under her body, so that the shape of her is a circle of creamy white. She'll move soon.)

For a while, she lay in the dog bed we'd purchased for her—orthopedic, expensive. Until we moved, and then it was only our bed—king-sized, also orthopedic, and now, perpetually covered in downy white hair. When we tell her to get off our bed, it doesn't matter the manner of hand gesture or voice command. She simply sits up long enough to rearrange herself, choose a more comfortable spot, and hide her muzzle among the pillows, ignoring us.

Every time I look at her, splayed out on my bed like an elegant—if bony—rug, I see him. She is as many years old as he is gone. The grief that motivated her purchase was once a fighter that picked its punches, catching me off guard, flattening me in a world impatient with the timeline of recovery.

Now it's a whisper that connects us both. Me and her. Him and me.

On February 8, 2014, my sister-in-law went to wake my brother Sam in their bed, and found he had succumbed to the ravages of lymphoma. Ten days before, he had called to wish me a happy fortieth birthday. "I'm so glad you were born," he had said.

He was thirty-six.

The next month, I told my husband, Matt, that I thought it was time to get another dog. "A Borzoi, please," I'd said. "I miss Gandalf."

The truth was, I missed Sam.

We'd put down Gandalf, our previous Borzoi, years earlier, and we'd all felt the vacuum of his loss. Gandalf had cut an imposing figure. A statuesque black-and-white guardian with an earth-shaking bark, he had once faced off against a bull that had escaped from the neighbor's cattle farm. He wasn't one for cuddling. He kept largely to himself, preferring the space of the unfinished basement to our company. The day we lost him, Matt, a hulking figure, had sobbed so that his body shook like a child's. Matt is not someone I would consider a "dog person," and he never particularly connected to Gandalf, so Matt's grief didn't seem rational to me. But then, grief rarely does.

Losing Gandalf, losing Sam. They were connected by my grief, and I longed for its antidote. I began to think about getting another dog. I wanted to love something new. I'd remembered the external manifestation of Matt's swallowing grief and thought somehow another canine companion would save us both.

(And now she is off the bed and under my feet at the computer, with her elongated nose pressed into the back of my foot. Notice me, she says.)

I told Matt, "A Borzoi . . . Just, you know, one of these days . . ."

We are now, after seventeen years of marriage, keen enough to realize that when one of us says "one of these days," it means we've already made up our minds.

But the reality of another dog would complicate our lives. We already had two. And we had three kids. We were living in a rented home and had brought three guinea pigs, two cats, a horse, a pony, and the dogs with us. Matt traveled for work, often leaving me alone with our family zoo. How we'd sell our landlord on the idea, I didn't know. That made no difference to Matt, who simply saw me hurting and set out to find a Borzoi breeder. He knew—he tells me now—that everything would work out. In its own way—neatly or otherwise, and mostly otherwise—everything always has.

But his was no easy task, looking for a large Russian sighthound in a suburbia dominated by labs and retrievers. We'd had only one conversation about a puppy. I dismissed the idea as a function of the temporary mania induced by sadness and didn't mention it again.

Two months later, Matt slid the computer over to me as we sat together at the kitchen table. On the screen was a checkerboard of puppy pictures in small frames. They were all colors. Steel gray, red with black masks, black with white paws. He pointed to one. Snow white with a pink nose peppered with black. The only white puppy in the litter. The only one not spoken for.

"Her name is Faith. She's coming on Saturday."

I grabbed his hand. "Faith?" I asked. "Faith, Faith, Faith," I repeated, hanging on the name like a mantra. I jumped up and wrapped myself around him.

In southern Virginia, near the town where my husband had grown up, a litter of Borzoi had been whelped on my birthday. On the day my brother called to tell me he was glad I'd been born, a litter of ten squirming hounds had also been born. It was the first litter from two dogs owned by a husband and wife who had begun a small breeding business after many years of struggling with their own infertility. Matt had spent weeks on the computer and phone, trying to find a match. Faith was the last available puppy from the litter. The breeders told him, "Faith is no shrinking violet. She likes to be noticed and needs lots of affection." Which was perfect, because I had more than enough to give.

(Now she is laying her long muzzle on the computer, forcing me to blow off the web-fine hairs and push her gently away. Pet me, she says. Her long, feathery tail swings low and slow.)

When that April Saturday came for her delivery, the breeders arrived with a white puppy and an armload of supplies. In a large pink bag that read "It's a girl!" was a blanket smelling like her littermates, a bag of dog food, and a squeaky toy (still her favorite). We never made it past the hallway—I sat down cross-legged on the floor, watching Faith explore her surroundings without fear or hesitation. Borzois are known to be reserved. They are generally shy with other dogs and people. Faith was neither.

After a few minutes of floor-sniffing, she walked over to me and climbed confidently into my lap, where she curled into a ball. I finally cried. I cried and cried, choking out something about how Faith had been the very thing I had prayed for. I cried about her sharing my birthday and her name reminding me that even grief is survivable. Out tumbled words about her color—bright white among the mottled landscape of her littermates—as though God had used it to point us to her, her uniqueness a reminder that he loved us and saw us in our loss.

The breeders handed me her AKC paperwork as Faith placed a long, floppy limb on my arm. Not knowing what any of it meant, I scanned the pedigree out of courtesy as I stroked Faith's downy head. Then I saw a name. One generation removed was Gandalf's sire.

Faith and Gandalf were related.

I watched Faith totter around the house on an unsteady tangle of limbs that day and for the next few weeks with so much happiness I nearly forgot my grief. Few things in my life have brought me as much joy as that dog. God knew in advance the events of February 8, 2014. So I believe he prepared us for the aftermath with the birth of a puppy beforehand. He pointed Matt directly to her in ways too notable to be coincidental. And her name was Faith so we would always be reminded of what God insists we endure but gives us the power to overcome.

(Downstairs, my children are tumbling in from school, and Faith is trying something of a howl that she has never quite developed to tell them she is upstairs. She wants to see them and trots to my office door, but she won't leave me. She flops herself back down at my feet, to wait for them and their embraces.)

Faith's breeders were right about her making her own way. She will delicately step onto the couch and insert herself between any two people as though she's a toy breed and not a giant one. She invades my office each day to shove her elongated snoot into my lap when I am in deepest thought. When she knows I am lying in bed, she will sprint to our room, take a flying leap onto the mattress, and once she's positioned herself, drop all of her eighty-five pounds on top of me.

But as a sighthound, she has sighthound eyes—big and dark and mournful. She doesn't look away when I stare at her, as many dogs would. She decisively meets my gaze, because there is something in her that sees beyond my exterior self. Our family has been blessed by many dogs over the years, and all have had their "person," their favorite. Faith and I will always be a matched set. We are bonded by the respite she gave me from a grief that seemed too much to bear.

Faith eats trash and litters our house with hair. She'd just as soon run the other direction as she would come when called. When we travel together in the car, she insists on trying to climb behind the steering wheel. Matt has said she's "dumb as a stump," to which I've reminded him that she's at least smart enough to use her height to reach food on the counter. Faith is big, obtrusive, and hairy. She will chase anything that moves but wouldn't think to warn us even if the house were on fire. In truth, there isn't much about her that's convenient.

But then grief—and love—rarely are.

Winnie Who Won Me Over

Susan Friedland-Smith

You should take her for a walk."

The foster mom of the beautiful red Doberman with natural ears handed me a leather leash. I snapped it onto the black collar of the dog that just might be "The One."

I felt apprehensive, not sure if I really knew how to walk a dog since I had never owned one, but as a lifelong horse lover, I knew how to lead horses around—it had to be similar, maybe even easier, right?

It was January in northern Illinois. I zipped my down jacket, pulled up the hood, looped my scarf around my neck, and grabbed my gloves, ready to face the white landscape with this dog named Winnie whom I might want to adopt. I had just moved back home to Illinois after living several years in California. I had my own apartment in Chicago, and it was dog friendly, which meant the time was right to plunge into dog ownership.

Moments before, when I knocked on the front door of the foster mom's house, five Dobermans appeared—all barking except one—the red one with floppy ears. She was Winnie.

I entered the house a little tentatively; I felt like I was on a first date. For the few months I had been searching dog rescue websites to find my perfect pet, I was also simultaneously searching for my human version of "The One," trying my hand at internet dating.

Winnie came to me when I sat down on the couch. She rested her chin on my leg, placed her right paw on my thigh, and gazed up at me. It was a look of adoration, longing, and intensity. I petted her and talked to her, feeling a little silly plopped down in someone's house I didn't know, breaking the ice with a dog.

I actually had my heart set on another dog I saw on the Illinois Doberman Rescue website. By the time my extensive paperwork had been reviewed and I was approved, the dog I had hoped to own, a black and tan female, had already been adopted. I was disappointed, since from her description, the black and tan dog seemed like my dream dog. The foster mom told me that I should consider Winnie, this red dog who was quiet and sweet, who liked to ride in the car, and enjoyed McDonald's hamburgers. Her husband had visited the drive-thru and decided if he was going to have a burger, it would only be fair to order Winnie one. She ate it with gusto.

As I scratched the smooth cinnamon crown of this two- or three-year-old dog's head—the veterinarian who examined her for the rescue couldn't determine her exact age—I learned she had been named Winnie after the Winnebago County Animal Shelter, where workers discovered her tied to the door wearing a Harley Davidson collar one morning. The shelter staff knew Winnie had been crate-trained because she wouldn't relieve herself in the cage. So the Doberman rescue was called to pick up "a very nice dog."

I walked Winnie down the block a ways, or I should say she walked me. It was not like leading a horse at all. Her auburn nose was pressed to the ground, and she trotted in zigzags following a special scent. I hoped none of the neighbors were looking out their windows, or they would have seen a cartoonish woman with a long scarf flying out behind her as she desperately tried to keep pace with a motivated dog.

After a quick tour up and down the suburban street that was coated with a thin layer of packed-down snow, Winnie and I made it back to the house. As we stood at the entry, I stomped the bottoms of my boots and leaned down to unsnap the leash.

"I'll take her."

I wrote a check for $200 for the adoption fee and set up an appointment to pick up Winnie the next weekend. I said good-bye to my new friend and told her I'd be back.

Once we were home together, Winnie instantly became my best friend. We walked my new neighborhood four times a day, drinking in the distinct seasons of the Midwest: winter's crunchy snow and inky skies, spring's greening transformation, summer's humid cloak and abundant sunshine, and fall's brisk air and the trees' vibrant fashion show. Winnie listened attentively as I shared with her my dating disappointments and how hard it was to adjust to my new yet familiar city.

Winnie and I went to obedience classes, where she excelled, like a straight-A student. She sat, shook hands, lay down, heeled, and came when called, as if she needed to set a good example for her canine classmates. On the last night of the series, the trainer brought out a maroon dog-sized cap and gown and took a Polaroid of my obedience graduate as I kneeled down next to her holding the diploma.

Chicago proved not to be a good fit for me, so after two years I returned to Los Angeles. Every summer we drove back to the Midwest to reunite with my family and friends. Winnie loved to travel. One year we traveled Route 66 together, stopping at most small towns' vintage attractions.

My rescue Doberman melted hearts wherever she went—even the hearts of people who did not consider themselves "dog people," like my own parents. Winnie's gentle demeanor and impeccable manners made her welcome in my mom's "no dogs allowed" home. In fact, soon after I adopted Winnie, my dad began buying dog treats to have on hand for this "dog of a lifetime" as he called her, after having only known her a couple of weeks. He loved to take her on power walks through their neighborhood.

Winnie was my "wing woman" on my first date with the man who would become my husband. I knew dogs were excellent judges of character, so it seemed appropriate to have Winnie accompany me for the first meet up over frozen yogurt. When we met on our blind date, Winnie greeted the tan man in white tennis clothes with metronome wags of her stubby brown tail. Winnie's quiet approval spoke volumes. Hours spent poring over profiles and the online communication back and forth proved fruitful in introducing me to both the dog and the man of my dreams.

It turned out that walking a dog was not as hard as I thought it might be. And it was a wonderful way to explore the neighborhood and the country, make new friends, and even sniff out a husband.

Dogs Know

Judy Auger, as told to Lauraine Snelling

I have always known dogs are smart, but I did not realize how much dogs know until I met Buffy.

I didn't plan for Buffy to come into my life—or rather our lives. My husband, Gerry, was very ill, his body shutting down bit by bit. For the last years, he had said "No dogs" because he was afraid of tripping over one. It seemed wise, so I agreed, thinking I would probably never have another dog. But that didn't seem important at the moment. Taking care of Gerry was.

And then Buffy showed up in our lives.

Our son's brother-in-law rescued a terrified, scruffy little dog at school. After failing to find an owner, he sent a picture of the dog to Jon and said, "Want this dog?"

Jon did not want her, but he knew who might. He contacted us with a photo of this move-into-your-heart dog and said, "Mom, Dad, I think this dog is supposed to be yours."

I said yes and then asked Gerry what he thought. After a short pause, he said with his lovely French accent, "Yes. We'll take this little dog."

It was a done deal. We acquired a dog. Scruffy is a name that would have fit her because of her appearance. Instead we decided on Buffy to fit in with Jon's dogs, whose names all started with the letter B.

Buffy looked scruffy, yes, but after a bath and grooming we realized she was also fluffy. She appeared to be a terrier mix, and she looked her best with a half cut so we could see her lovely brown spots and one little black dot on her white body. Her long feathery tail was as fluffy as the rest of her, and it wagged and wagged and wagged.

Buffy grew into her legs and body in the months after she came to live with us, and as she grew we learned she was fast. She possessed unbounded energy and a lightning quick tongue that licked anyone within licking distance. She could zip around faster than any dog that I'd ever seen, and I suspected maybe there was some greyhound in her. She had a little mustache and a bit of an overbite. Her warm, dark brown eyes seemed to say, "Hey, I'm yours, and I am dee-lighted!"

And from the first moment, she glued herself to Gerry.

Now, in the past, our dogs have pretty much been mine because I took care of them. But Gerry needed her, and this was when I began to understand how dogs "know." She never left his side, and he kept his hand on her all the time. That was so unlike Gerry. Buffy was energy in motion unless she was with Gerry— sitting in his lap, lying in his lap, sleeping in his lap, sleeping next to him, with him—and always loving him with those warm eyes and lightning tongue.

After Buffy arrived, Gerry steadily weakened in a matter of only months. Hospice came in to help us, but he didn't live much longer. Buffy stayed right beside him until the men carried his body out.

In the following days, she searched the house for Gerry. Then she attached herself to me. She looked at me with those compassionate eyes, and I felt like she was saying, "Okay, Mom. We're in this together. It's okay. It's going to be okay." And I knew it would be because Gerry was so ready to go home.

Now Buffy knew that I was the needy one.

So as my life as a widow began, the dance of grief began. One step forward, sometimes two back. It is a slow dance. But it's easier with a dog.

Buffy loves everyone, but she takes care of me. She makes sure I get enough exercise, so we walk—a lot. She makes sure that I bend over because she isn't quite all the way housebroken yet, or at least she wasn't until lately. It's easy when you're a widow and trying to learn to live all over again to forget to cook or even eat. But Buffy makes sure that I eat because she makes sure that she eats. She makes sure that I get rest. I'm a restless sleeper, but she knows I should be lying still because she can sleep better when I'm lying still. So I do, and then, amazingly, I sleep.

She reminds me to laugh as she zips around our house or a friend's house, down the halls, over the furniture, under the table around me—and repeat. Perhaps even again. Laughter is like applause to her. She skids to a stop in front of me and preens her pride.

And now, amazingly, the first and they say the hardest year has passed. Buffy and I have been through all the holidays, the special family days, and the horrendous amount of paperwork required even when the affairs were all in order. Glitches happen. Tears still attack, try to drown me at times.

But I have learned, mostly from others who have lost a loved one, that this is all the normal part of the dance. Buffy dries my tears and needs me like I need her. She is my constant companion, and she goes almost everywhere with me. She is a gift I had no idea how much I would need. But she knew. As I said, dogs know.

Beautifully Imperfect

Xochitl E. Dixon

I fought back tears as my kindergartener pleaded his case to his father. Xavier held up a packet of papers. "Mom helped me do research," he said. "We want a beagle. They hardly shed at all, Daddy."

My husband, Alan, glared at me. "It doesn't matter how much they shed. We're not ready for another dog. I don't know if we'll ever be ready."

Xavier turned his hopeful big brown eyes toward me. His scarred smile mocked me.

It's your fault. All your fault.

The year before, overcome with impatience, I'd insisted we adopt a friendly adult golden Labrador from a family we knew nothing about. By the time we realized the dog had been abused by his previous owners, my son lay strapped to a table in the local children's hospital under the care of a plastic surgeon. I'd knelt by Xavier's head, comforting him as a single tear slipped down his cheek. How would I ever forgive myself for not protecting my boy? How would I ever make things right?

Xavier had insisted we forgive Buddy, even though the dog had to leave our home. But I had a hard time forgiving that dog, as I secured a boulder of blame on my back.

So, when Xavier presented his position with a hard-to-refuse, one-front-tooth-missing grin, my momma-heart longed to keep him smiling . . . even though I could never make the scar disappear.

"We don't have to make a decision today," I said. "But we can at least pray about it."

Xavier scrambled off his chair. "Let's start now." He placed his small hands on his dad's broad shoulders. "Lord, please help us find a dog that's licky, fetchy, cuddly, but not bitey."

We repeated this prayer before bed every night until, two years later, Xavier received a call from his godfather, who claimed to have found us a beagle.

After a quick family huddle, we set out to divide and conquer. Xavier and his dad shopped for pet supplies while I drove, cash in hand, to pick up our new pup.

When I pulled into The Godfather's driveway, he waved me into the house and led me to the garage. I frowned at the lump of fur sprawled on a burgundy towel next to a rumbling washing machine. The pup lay still, sporting all the right colors. Black. Brown. White. Patched. But the mutt in the corner was *not* the promised purebred I'd expected. I turned toward The Godfather. "That's not a beagle."

He shrugged. "The mom is." He scooped up the pup and thrust her into my arms. "She's cute."

"But she's . . ."

"I know. I know. Not a beagle."

Just as I prepared to back out of the deal, the pup licked my face. *Great. I've been chosen.* She closed her eyes, snuggled into my shoulder, and pressed her cool, wet nose against my neck. Her whimper melted my resistance. "It's not like I can go home empty-handed after promising my kid a puppy," I said, forking over the agreed-upon finder's fee.

I waved good-bye, feeling a bit ripped off, and placed the pooch in the passenger seat. She scratched her ear with her hind leg, sending fur flying in all directions. *Nice. She's a shedder.* Still, her tongue-curling yawn tugged on my heart. Fretting over her obvious imperfections, I tried convincing myself that it wouldn't matter if she wasn't a purebred. She seemed to be everything we'd asked for during our two years of praying and waiting. Licky. Cuddly. Okay, so she didn't look very fetchy. Silver lining? At least lethargic dogs are less likely to be bitey. I hoped.

As I pulled into our driveway, Xavier gave me a hand-clapping welcome.

Alan's mustache twitched. "This is *not* a beagle."

I shrugged. "The mom is."

He tucked the so-not-a-beagle under one arm, then plucked a few strands of white fur from my shirt. "She sheds . . . a lot."

Xavier stroked the pup's silky, pancake ears. "She's ours, right?"

After a few puppy kisses, Alan nodded and led our family to the backyard.

The once-lethargic pooch trailed her boy, quick as a greyhound. When she slowed to a prance, her ears and tongue flapped.

I smiled. "She looks like she's dancing. Let's call her Prancer. Or how about Flapper?"

Alan sank deep into his plastic lawn chair. "Let's name her Jazzy."

Xavier lay belly down on the lush grass. "C'mon, Jazzy," he said, burying his face in his arms. He giggled as the pup hopped over and around his head. "She likes her name, Mom."

"Of course she does," I said. "It's perfect."

My boy had a dog. He didn't mind if she shed too much. He didn't care if she wasn't a purebred. She was his. He was hers. Nothing else mattered, until later that day when we discovered the reason Jazzy had been lethargic. Flea infestations can cause anemia in dogs.

Upset that the previous owner had allowed our pup to be put at risk and said nothing, we scrubbed and pinched plump fleas from her fur. That night, Jazzy faithfully gave each of us equal cuddle time, as if she knew we'd saved her life.

A couple of years later, we discovered the extent of Jazzy's resilience when a little-boy-knee-to-canine-head accident resulted in her near-fatal head injury.

It happened during a weekly Bible study at our house, during which Xavier entertained the kids in the backyard. I'd repeatedly warned the backyard explorers to steer clear of the fence that separated our yard from Bandito's. After years of my loving our neighbor's Jack Russell terrier with extra cuddles and doggie treats, he'd proven he could and would hop the fence to guard our yard.

A flurry of barking and kids screaming affirmed the backyard bunch had ignored my warnings. I leapt out of my chair and dashed into the yard. The pint-sized reporters admitted they'd ventured too close to Bandito's fence. When he hopped high enough to peer over the barrier between him and the trespassers, the kids screamed, and Jazzy raced to their rescue. As our heroic hound rounded the corner, she collided headfirst with Xavier's knee. She wasn't expected to survive, but she did.

I served as her nurse and comforted her while she recovered. The permanent indentation above her left eye reminds me of the cracked skull that almost took her away from us. We thank God for sparing our miracle mutt and for using her to love us for over a decade and still counting after her injury. I'm grateful for the opportunities I've had to show her love by caring for her when she was in great need.

In 2012, our resilient rescue dog returned the favor and became my nurse.

An old injury, worsened by my overcompensation to minimize hurting, thrust me into a healing journey that has tested my faith in ways I could never have imagined possible. I've been house-bound, suffering from chronic pain daily. I've battled depression and felt isolated. I've struggled with feeling useless and alone, as my husband and now grown son work full-time and share the load as my caregivers.

When I'm overwhelmed, lonely, or in the middle of a mini emotional meltdown, Jazzy licks away my tears. When I'm feeling forgotten or sorry for myself, my twenty-six-pound lapdog cuddles my sorrow away. She's a patient Bible prop and the best writing buddy I've ever had. She hasn't learned how to fetch my slippers, but she loves playing fetch and she's not bitey. So, I can't complain.

To this day, Jazzy checks on Xavier when he's sleeping, making sure her boy is safe as she provides an abundance of love-licks. She follows Alan around whenever he's home, most content when resting at her daddy's feet. But my miracle mutt spends the bulk of her days remaining close to me, a furry reminder that God hasn't forgotten me as I trust him through the toughest days of my suffering.

Jazzy nudges my hand so I can pet her when I'm having a rough day. She chases her tail, offering a doggie grin when I reward her with a laugh . . . and a bacon-flavored tasty snack.

She isn't the purebred we originally wanted. She's got a cracked skull and sheds a lot. But when I think about all the years she's spent loving and caring for us, it doesn't seem like she's the only one who was rescued. She needs us. But we need her too. More than we asked for and all we truly needed, this beautifully imperfect pup was and is a perfect fit for our family.

The Great Jazzy Rescue

Dr. W. Alan Dixon, Sr.

After almost ten years working for the same company, I found myself unemployed for the first time in nearly thirty years. The company restructure shook the stability of my income and my confidence. Being the sole provider for my family was only the first part of my concern. My wife was undergoing multiple medical procedures requiring benefits. I needed to find a new job with good benefits, quickly.

As I applied for countless jobs, our nine-year-old dog, Jazzy, lay on the floor right by my side. I brought her bed into my office so she could be more comfortable. Jazzy was always a good dog, but I never really connected with her until my forced time at home. I was good at hiding my concern from my family, all the while deeply worried about my rapidly depleting funds and lack of job opportunities. But Jazzy knew something was wrong with her daddy.

I was facing one of the most challenging times of my life. I had no way to support my family, and I didn't know when this situation would end. Though in my heart I knew God had a plan for me, it was hard to trust through all the constant rejections. On those difficult days when I could not stand reading another denial, Jazzy would look up at me with understanding eyes. She would gaze at me for a moment as if she were saying everything would be okay.

For ten months, Jazzy remained by my side as I took new and unexpected journeys. Up until then, she had been more attached to my wife and son; I'd never spent much time with Jazzy. Now for the first time in her life, Daddy was home every day. And for the first time in my life, I was not working.

I did not understand why I had to experience joblessness. Yet, I remember my wife for years asking when was I going to slow down so I could experience and enjoy the life going on around me. To be honest, if the restructure hadn't forced me to hit the brakes, I had no intention of ever slowing down. I used to joke with my wife and say, "I'll sleep when I'm dead." She never thought that was funny.

During those ten months of job searching, I could do something I had not done in almost thirty years, except for on the occasional vacation. I slept in. There was Jazzy, snuggling up to me, as if she were giving me her silent approval. *It's okay to rest, Daddy.* I found myself working and periodically taking naps throughout the day, between job searches. Right by my side was Jazzy, snoozing. When we weren't napping or job searching, we found ourselves just hanging out, playing tug of rope or fetch. She would play until she was tired and then go to her bed or jump on my lap and take some time to rest.

During my ten-month sabbatical, I spent more time with my family and spent a lot of extra time with my dog. When I left my office, Jazzy would wake up out of a deep sleep and follow me around the house. My wife told me Jazzy waited at the door when I was out running errands or playing softball. My dog just wanted to be near her daddy.

In one of the toughest times in my life, I found myself growing stronger in my faith. And I believe that God used my dog to show me how to appreciate the best gift I could ever receive . . . rest. I failed to understand how important simple rest was until I had an abundance of it. Searching for jobs was stressful. However, when my frustration peaked, Jazzy would come to me and paw my hand until I petted her or let her jump onto my lap.

After ten months, what I consider a miracle happened. We were down to our last $70. The husband of my former office assistant gave my name to a recruiter. I was sitting in my office, while Jazzy snored in her bed, when my phone rang. Normally, I did not answer unfamiliar numbers, but for some reason I felt compelled to answer this call. An hour later, I had a phone interview. The following day, I drove to the airport to have an in-person interview. Then . . . silence.

A week passed, and I still had not heard back. I figured I didn't get the job, so I called the recruiter to ask what I could have done differently. The recruiter told me that not only did I get the job, I had to fly to Los Angeles for orientation the next day. I could not believe I had just landed a job I had not even applied for.

When I lost my job, I felt lost and in need of rescue. For the first time, I was unemployed and had no idea of what I was going to do. I had been running myself into the ground with work. Getting rest—and getting closer to my God, my family, and even my dog—were not on my radar.

God had other plans. He used our dog, Jazzy, to rescue me from myself.

Finding the Way Home

Denise Fleck

D ay settled into twilight as the sun bowed to the stars, and crickets chirped nonstop. I, a young girl of ten with blonde pigtails, sat alone cross-legged on the dock with a mangled mess of fishing line before me.

Earlier my friends had huddled around with their legs dangling over the dock's edge and their fishing poles cast toward the sparkling lake. Several four-legged creatures had enjoyed the sights and smells with us as well. A scruffy-eared German shepherd kept causing a ruckus as he dashed after the tabby-striped cat who kept sneaking onto the dock for an easy fish dinner. Two Chihuahua brothers sat quietly to one side grooming each other while a yellow-and-white shepherd mix visited each of us one at a time, begging for ear scratches and belly rubs.

But it was now well past dinnertime, and the aroma of cooked meals had already faded from the breeze. Everyone had gone home while I sat, close to tears, still trying unsuccessfully to untangle the knotted mess of fishing line.

While struggling, my mind flashed to Blondie, a new stray dog in the neighborhood who had recently started following us kids around. Weighing in at about seventy pounds, she was a young female, white and yellow, possibly part shepherd and part yellow Labrador retriever with a loving and gentle personality. She was "in heat," my mom told us, and a neighbor remembered seeing her chase a green VW Bug the first time he saw her. Sadly, her owners must not have wanted to deal with the responsibilities of her seasonal situation and had abandoned her.

Blondie seemed drawn to me. I, with my mom's blessing but much to my dad's dismay, snuck the dog into the garage one rainy night. Although my dad loved animals, he was not yet ready to take another one in after the recent and very painful loss of our beloved Great Dane. Dad didn't want to become attached.

For several days, Blondie, as the neighborhood had named her because of her coloring, followed my entourage to the lake, swimming out to the sandbar only to have us hold her up in the too-deep water while she attempted to tread water doggie-style. Blondie would lie in the grass when we played softball, often beating the outfielders to their prized catch. Then for the next several minutes, the game would come to a halt as the two-legged players would chase their four-legged rival for the now slobbery ball. Afterwards, she could be found right alongside us as we followed the jingling sound of the ice cream truck, and on several occasions Blondie was even seen stealing a cone or two!

Bringing my thoughts back to the situation at hand, I started crying as I wiped the bangs off my forehead in exasperation. How I wished my beloved Blondie were here to comfort me. I could pet her soft forehead and all would be right with the world again. I knew my parents would be worried that I wasn't home by curfew, but I just couldn't carry my fishing gear home in its muddled state down the long dock and several streets to my home.

As I figured and would learn later, my mom and dad were becoming quite concerned about their only child who, until now, had always been prompt in returning home once the sun set. All of the neighborhood parents had sundown curfews for their kids with exceptions made only on those rare evenings when the fireflies beckoned and a game of flashlight tag was in order.

After nearly wearing out a path in the living room carpet, my anxious dad came out onto his raised backyard deck where, if the sunny day hadn't already turned into night, he could have seen the lake in the distance. Below he spied a shadow in the grass that stretched out in a sleepless rest.

"Blondie?" he called. "Where's Denise, girl? Can you show me?"

Blondie sprang to her four feet, stretched, yawned, and wagged her tail before running with the speed of the wind toward the lake. Every few seconds, she looked back and returned to my dad, encouraging him to follow. That he did, and after a spirited jaunt, Blondie led him through the narrow side yard entrance of a neighbor's lakeside home. Down a grassy embankment, Blondie moved easily in the dark and onto the long rickety dock lit only by the light of the waxing moon.

At the end of the dock, I sat surprised and delighted to suddenly be slobbered upon with doggie kisses. Embarrassed, I looked up at my dad and began to stutter, worried he would be angry with me for being out so late.

Instead, though, he scooped me into his arms with a sigh of relief. "I'm so glad you're okay," he said.

He helped gather all my things, grabbed my hand, and walked me home, led by the golden dog.

As we reached the door to our home, I paused to kneel down and kiss and pat Blondie's head good night.

But my dad stopped me and said, "Let Blondie come in. She certainly earned herself a comfortable night's sleep."

Later that evening, just before I drifted off to sleep with Blondie curled on a rug next to my bed, I heard my dad come in. I cracked one eye open the tiniest amount, and I saw him reward Blondie with a biscuit and an extra special belly rub.

"Thank you, Blondie," he said, "for bringing my little girl home. You have a forever home with us if you want it."

Blondie licked his hand, wagged her tail, and drifted off to sleep with a smile on her face. My daddy smiled too, and my heart got warm inside knowing I once again would have a furry best friend by my side.

It Started with a Guinea Pig

Missy Tippens

It started with a trip to Petco that fateful day fourteen years ago when I reluctantly took my excited children—ages thirteen, eight, and six—to buy a guinea pig. We already had a beautiful two-year-old chocolate Lab and two persnickety cats. I dreaded the thought of another animal to feed, but I *had* promised them, after all. Besides, how much trouble could one little guinea pig be?

Warning: Do not go to pet stores on adoption day. Not unless you're prepared to fall in love.

When we entered the pet shop, we discovered it was adoption day. Clusters of people filled normally empty spaces, and yaps and barks punctuated the air. Before we could work our way over to the rodents, we ran into the puppies. Lots of them. And in one fenced-off area, we spotted three precious siblings. The one that caught my eye (and the eye of two of my children) was a sweet white spotted dog with a black patch of fur around his eye, a shiny black nose and lips, and silky black ears. He was curled up, sound asleep. Utterly precious.

Of course, my kids hurried to ask if we could wake him and hold him, and the volunteer was happy to hand him to us. The cute little thing woke up bright-eyed, wiggled to get down, and promptly tinkled on the floor. Then he started to play with the kids, loving every minute of the attention.

We were goners.

The poor little thing had been found with his litter, abandoned on the side of a road. A foster mom had been taking care of them, but now he needed a permanent home. The kids begged to get him instead of the guinea pig. I thought long and hard and wavered on bringing another dog into the family. But once I called my husband to let him know of the situation, I realized we had fallen in love, and there was no way we could leave the little guy behind. After extracting a promise from the kids that they would do all the doggie care and feeding, I finally agreed. We adopted our new puppy.

John. His name was John.

On the way home, we quickly decided his name didn't fit. After much discussion, we rejected the suggestion from my six-year-old of calling him Cookies 'n Cream, because we couldn't imagine going out to the backyard and calling, "Here, Cookies 'n Cream, come inside, Cookies 'n Cream!" We decided on Duke. Definitely more manageable. Of course, the fact that Duke University was my oldest son's dream college influenced the decision—not to mention, he could be very persuasive with his little brother and sister.

So Duke became a part of our family and became especially attached to me. To help him through the night those first weeks as he grieved leaving his siblings, I slept on the couch with him on my chest. The poor thing acted starved each time we fed him. I guess he'd had to fight for every scrap of food before being rescued by the foster family. Gradually, he learned to trust us, to trust that his tummy would always be full.

As the years passed and he settled into adulthood, he learned to sit by my feet (or on top of them!) as I worked on my laptop writing my books. A faithful companion, he lovingly kept my feet warm during the winter and . . . well, during all seasons, whether I needed the heat or not. My kids always teased me about how adoringly Duke would look into my eyes. I often told my buddy how fortunate he was to have been adopted by a family that spoiled him rotten and that loved him so much.

Several years ago, we had a scare when we found out he had a tumor in his leg muscle. The biopsy showed it was malignant. We opted to do surgery and go through the long recovery. With prayer, we waited to find out whether it had clear margins. It didn't. Finally, after one more surgery, we got the good news that they'd gotten all the cancer. My writing companion would be fine.

As the children grew up, one by one they left home to attend college. When the youngest left home, my husband and I had a tough time with the empty nest. Our home that had always been bustling with activity stood quiet. And while my husband was at work each day, I found myself knocking around the house, trying to find my new place in the world after being a stay-at-home mom with a home-based business. On some of the difficult days, I found myself comforted by the beautiful brown eyes and silky black ears of Duke, who still needed me.

Nowadays, when I look into his eyes, that precious black patch of fur around his eye interspersed with white, I don't tell him that he's so very lucky to have found our family. No, I'm more likely to gaze at him and thank him for being my companion when I needed him most. Sure, I may gripe that he has to be taken outside more often now in his old age. I may worry about leaving him outside when it's cold now that he's growing into a bony old man. But I love him, and he loves me, and we have a nice understanding that I still need him to warm my toes while I write.

I'll be forever grateful that when we went looking to buy a guinea pig fourteen years ago, we happened upon a puppy, one who needed me as much as I would one day need him.

From Stray to College Professor

Sandra Murphy

The day I met Izzie, we had a once-in-awhile St. Louis ice storm that left thick, shiny layers of slickness over the steps, the car, the trees, and, well, everything. I decided I had to have the Sunday newspaper for the comics and puzzles since I was going to be stuck inside for who knew how long. For once, the newspaper was near the front steps, where I could reach it. My shoes would be too slick but my socks would stick to the ice better, giving me some traction. It would only take a minute. I eased my way out the door and down a couple of steps.

There she was—a midsized terrier-ish dog with a big smile on her face, in spite of the fact that she was sitting on the ice floe that was my front yard. She was tricolored and had one ear up, one ear down. I'd seen her in the neighborhood before. I'm not as observant as I should be or I'd have figured out earlier that the people she walked with were never the same ones twice. She'd just fall in behind and walk them home, hoping it would be her home too, I guess. Luckily for me, it never was. Once when the neighborhood kids watched me try to catch her, they asked, "Is he your dog?" Those first two words came out like "Izzie." I decided then and there, if she ever was my dog, her name would be Izzie. This was my chance.

I tossed little bites of treats to her as I inched my way down the icy steps. The treats were running low as I neared the bottom. I took a chance and dropped the last one near my feet. When she bent her head down to grab it, I picked her up and snagged the newspaper. It's a good thing she had such a great temperament, since that put her face-to-face with me. I tucked her under one arm before either of us could panic and headed back up the steps, hanging on to the railing and the newspaper for dear life with the left hand and keeping a tight grip on Izzie with the right. Somehow we made it without any embarrassing incidents.

Once inside, I plopped her on the floor, and she ran upstairs to hide. I sat in the middle of the living room floor to thaw out and read the comics. My back was to the stairs, but I had a good view of them in the mirror over the mantel. She crept down the stairs, a little at a time. It took her almost an hour for the twelve-step trip. She stood in the doorway for a few minutes. I didn't dare move. I heard her nails click across the hardwood. She nudged the comics out of the way and climbed into my lap and into my heart.

Izzie liked most other dogs but had a problem with big Labrador types. I think she must have been bullied by such dogs as a stray. To get her over her fears, we enrolled in an obedience class. I was nervous about the final exam, but Izzie took it in stride. She learned to heel on mats laid out in a square over carpet. Dogs were to walk on the mats. One of the last tests was for her to sit and stay. She sat at one corner. I crossed to the opposite side and gave the command, "Izzie, come!" She jumped up, started to cross the floor, then stopped and looked the situation over. Apparently, one was not supposed to walk across the carpeted inner square but stay on the mats—at least to her way of thinking. It was all we could do not to erupt in laughter as she very carefully walked from her corner to the next and to me via an L-shaped route, never touching carpet.

We signed up for another class, and then the tricks class, and that led to her learning to be a therapy dog on a team. She loved to visit kids and residents from the nearby retirement home. One of her favorite residents was Miss Dorothy, who as a child had been bitten by a dog and was afraid of them for the rest of her life—until she met Izzie. After Miss Dorothy broke her hip, Izzie sat on the edge of the bed and let the woman hold her paw and talk for over an hour.

We did a demonstration at Grant's Farm, the former home of Ulysses S. Grant and now a tourist attraction, complete with animals. Izzie was brave in most situations, but when she saw horses for the first time, she couldn't believe those big things could move around. Her friend, Miles, a golden retriever, loved horses and walked right up for a nose touch. Izzie was appalled. With Miles's encouragement, she army-crawled to the fence and reached up for a nose touch too. The second that was over, she raced back to me. "I did it!" was all over her face.

I'm not that good a trainer, but with Izzie, I could say, "This is what I want you to do, can you do that?" I'd show her a trick or a dance move—we were on a drill team by then—and she'd mimic me. She also invented her own tricks. I told her heel meant have your head right by my knee. Our back sidewalk was very narrow with only room for one of us on it. She decided she shouldn't walk on the grass, but there wasn't room on the concrete. To solve the problem, she stepped behind me, stuck her head between my knees, and heeled. We called it "tween," and it was a popular trick.

When Izzie got older and then was very ill, she never let it get her down. During the years, I bragged about her online, so she had friends around the world. They followed Izzie's life, and they followed her illness too. We went to the University of Missouri at Columbia Veterinary School (Mizzou) for treatment. They're a teaching hospital so students rotate in and out of the oncology department. I told Izzie we were there to teach them.

When we received the news that there was no more to be done for Izzie, I practiced my speech at home about a hundred times so I could say it without crying. At our next appointment, I said, "Izzie comes here to teach her students. She'd like to continue to do that. Is there a way for her to do like my Uncle Bill did and leave her body to science?"

Dr. Bryan, our oncologist, was almost too enthused to hear the news. Most of the time they never see the animals again after they pass away. To do a necropsy (an autopsy on an animal) would be a great teaching tool.

Don't ever let anybody tell you how long a dog has to live. Izzie beat Dr. Bryan's estimate by several weeks. I had been giving her subcutaneous fluids, which helped. After a joint birthday party with her dog buddy Beau on Saturday, she let me know she was done with treatment. On Monday, I called Dr. Bryan to say we were coming for our final visit. I ran one errand and returned home to find Izzie had left without me.

Since I wanted her illness to be a teaching tool, I still made the trip. During the necropsy, the veterinarians took tissue samples, which remain on file in perpetuity. I find comfort in the sound of that. If there's a promising cancer cure, they can test it on her samples.

Dr. Bryan lectures at other veterinary teaching hospitals as well as medical conferences for humans. Izzie travels with him as part of his PowerPoint presentation. I told him he has to tell her story, from stray to therapy dog, so students see she's more than a tissue sample on a slide. She was my therapy partner, my friend, and my family. Her grinning face is one of the first slides shown.

Izzie also has a scholarship at Mizzou to be given to a student with an interest in oncology. It pays for one of the more expensive books. Her story is included inside the front cover.

We say Izzie is teaching at Mizzou now, a professor emeritus. You'd think that would be enough for a little dog to do, but no, she had another idea in mind—or at least that's what I believe.

Izzie must have decided that I'd be at loose ends with no therapy visits or training to do, so she thought up another career for me. I've been in retail management, supervised teamster truck drivers, and created and sold jewelry. Now I needed something more. I'd been pet-sitting too, and one night it came to me as one of my clients, beagle Jackson Newman, snoozed on my lap. I wished someone had told me what to expect when Izzie got sick—I should write about it to tell others. Poor Jackson Newman got a rude awakening as I jumped up to make notes right then, before I could forget.

I came up with twelve things—wrote, polished, and rearranged them. Then I had a writer friend look them over and make suggestions. I stalked the magazine section at Barnes and Noble to find the right magazine to send it to, which turned out to be *Animal Wellness*. Finally, one Tuesday afternoon, I took the plunge and hit send to zip the article off to their Canadian offices.

The next morning, I had an acceptance email. It took fifteen months to publish, since they wanted it for a special issue, but that was fine. In the meantime, I wrote out other ideas. I've written for *Animal Wellness* for years now and have added other magazines to the list. I'm considered an SME—subject matter expert—on pets and wildlife as well as eco-friendly green topics. I keep busy.

I never thought I'd be one of those people who would adopt a dog sight unseen, but I now have a Westie-ish boy named Ozzie. It's not a play on Izzie. I just saw his picture and said his name is Ozzie and he's my dog. He traveled from Dyersburg, Tennessee, with his rescuers, Miss Linda and the Captain, who had introduced me to him via email. He's smart and funny, and he makes up his own tricks, like the sit up/wave he does in his version of the hula when he hears the theme music for *Hawaii Five-O*.

Izzie was with me for twelve years. She gave me love and joy. Now she's teaching at Mizzou. Thanks to her, I'm writing about animals and the planet, and just maybe she sent Ozzie to supervise me. That's a lot, coming from a tricolored midsized terrier with one ear up, one ear down, and a great big smile.

Dozer Rescues Olaf

Maggie Sabatier-Smith

H e licked my hair!"

Dozer, a sixty-pound American bulldog, jumped up on my bench to look out the window. He was so grateful for the spot that he decided to lick my hair in appreciation.

Silly boy. Theoretically, he was here at this women's prison to learn obedience and good manners, as part of the Heel to Heal Dog Training & Rescue Program. Instead, this rambunctious two-year-old had mastered the art of "look how cute I am" and the ability to make us all smile and often crack up in laughter. Pure joy on the compound—not only for the inmates but for the officers and visitors too.

As a seasoned prison ministry volunteer, I found it to be a special treat to see Dozer every two weeks when I showed up to mentor my two ladies. One of my mentees was his handler, and she would bring Dozer to our mentoring sessions. This young dog was there for an eight-week program, and he won my heart. It was quite a challenge to stay focused as he would not sit still. Admittedly, it crossed my mind that it would be fun to have him join Beagle Bailey, our eight-year-old beagle basset rescue, as part of our family.

But seriously, what would my husband and I do with two dogs when we traveled cross-country in our RV? Regardless, I would often imagine what it would be like to take Dozer home with us. Beagle Bailey, a professional couch potato, would certainly be challenged into more activity by Dozer. But one of the officers had already agreed to adopt him upon graduation. Oh well. Although my heart had grown to make room for him, it was not to be.

Only days before his graduation, Dozer's handler frantically asked if I might be interested in adopting him. Apparently, the officer had reneged on the adoption. It was urgent Dozer be adopted upon graduation or he would be sent back to the animal shelter and, well . . . that could be the end of Dozer. Because of my relationship with him, he would be mine if I wanted. I said I would pray about it over the weekend.

Although it would be quite an adjustment, my husband and I agreed to adopt Dozer. We submitted the paperwork on Sunday night and would have to wait several days before we could bring him home. Excited, we began to anticipate the changes to our lifestyle to accommodate a more active member. I was surprised at how deeply I cared for Dozer. I couldn't wait to bring him to his forever home.

Two days later, however, the adoption fell through. The original officer decided he wanted the dog after all. I was heartbroken about this abrupt ending to our next adventure. I rationalized that it was God's will since, after all, we had prayed about it, hadn't we? I tried to convince myself that I was at peace with the outcome. Dozer had a forever home; he would be safe.

But stuffing my feelings lasted for a few days until I finally realized I was grieving the loss. Can you grieve a pet you never *really* owned? Yes, I could. Dozer had resurrected the playful, silly side of Maggie. My days of caregiving for my parents had been over for a few years and I had not realized how much I missed being needed—missed stepping up to do the extraordinary for someone.

The next Saturday morning, my husband said, "Let's go rescue our next pet." I'm sure if God had blessed me with a tail, I would have been wagging it and possibly licking Paul's face (not much hair to lick on his head).

Off we went to visit the local shelters.

We decided we would look for a Labrador mix—a dog similar to Willow, our black Lab who had passed away two years earlier. First stop, SPCA—no Labs, and a large white Dozer-like dog who was not friendly at all. Next, the County Animal Shelter, where we found a beautiful, energetic yellow Lab. But he was too young for us. And did I mention ADHD? He was everywhere, and nowhere. I imagined him settling down for the night in our motor home . . . No, I couldn't imagine that at all. Just *too* much energy.

We were almost ready to give up when we discovered that a Humane Society had opened a location nearby, and they had a Lab. *Yes!*

At the immaculate brand-new facility, we were escorted to the dog area. As usual, I bolted through the door first, and there he was three feet away . . . the funniest-looking fifty-pound white boxer with blue eyes. His ears moved in such a way that I was sure he was sending me a coded message. I said to the attendant, "This is a setup, isn't it? You put him up front because you know he will capture the heart of anyone who walks in."

Smiling and focused, she took us back to where the requested Lab was. He was a bundle of energy—so much so that he had a special door to his roommate's cage so the two of them could play to exhaustion. This would not do for us.

Determined not to return home empty-handed, I made my way around the cages, praying that I would be open to the one who needed us most—who would fit in with our family and who would fill in the empty places of my heart.

171

Who was I kidding? That first dog was the one—it was love at first sight with the white boxer. We joined him in the play area, where he was making hilarious faces and wagging his short-cropped tail. I couldn't stop smiling. He was a senior, just like the rest of our family. At eight and a half years old, he had been adopted and returned. He'd been waiting for the last six months.

Olaf jumped on to the back seat of our car as if he had ridden there forever. At home, Beagle Bailey gave him a welcome sniff of approval and returned to his bed. It took us about three interesting weeks to settle into our new normal. We were told he was "crate friendly." I'm sure there's a clear definition of what the organization meant by that, but it didn't match our expectation. He panicked when he was left in the crate for any length of time. We would return home to a clean-up job. But once he realized he would not be abandoned, all crate issues went away. Thank goodness!

We have discovered Olaf is a talker. Yes, a welcome surprise. He gives a friendly, low, almost melodious growl when he wants something. He has become my shadow, finding comfy spots wherever I am, especially under my desk—as I write this, Olaf and Beagle Bailey are both there. Our only challenge has been his non-relationship with Hey-Kitty-Kitty, our indoor/outdoor cat. She likes to stay on the porch, and Olaf is *not welcome there*. We often find them nose-to-nose with a sliding glass door between them . . . that's as close as they choose to be.

As for our RV adventures, that has yet to be tested. Perhaps that will be my next story: "The Beagle Bailey & Olaf Adventures."

Dozer rekindled my need to be silly and playful. He resurrected my laughter. And Dozer prepared the way for us to meet Olaf. We can't imagine life without Olaf now. No matter the challenges, we will make it work. We're family.

Empty Arms
but Not Empty Heart

Cyle Young

All of my life I dreamed of having a Weimaraner for a pet. Most people call them "Weims" because they can't pronounce the German word, but I like to call the beautiful silver-gray dogs with velvety fur Weimies. These affectionate animals have large flat ears, and you typically see them dressed up as humans and photographed for calendars by the famous photographer William Wegman.

I'm not ashamed. I dressed mine up too, and Miss Holly Berry loved every second of it.

For our first Christmas together, my wife and I went to the pet store and purchased an eight-week-old bundle of joy. Since it was the holidays, we decided to name her after the season. We chose the name Holly Berry. Yes, it's a play on the name of the famous actress Halle Berry. We added the "Miss" because Holly was destined to become a show dog champion. I had carefully planned out Holly's future and set her on a path to one day prance around during the Thanksgiving Day televised National Dog Show.

That day never came. But it wasn't Holly's fault. I hired a trainer for her, and she attended dog obedience classes. The trainer worked with her on walking with a proper gait and standing in the appropriate posing position. When Holly was ready, I paid for the trainer to take her to a few dog shows. There she won some awards, but she never seemed to have the success I'd envisioned.

The main reason her dog show career stalled was because of *me*.

When Holly was a puppy, I babied her. She slept in our bed. We were together constantly, and I carried her everywhere. She rode on my lap in the car. But as cute as that can be for a six-pound puppy, it's not healthy for a sixty-pound adult Weimaraner. Imagine driving with a large dog in your lap—the turns are tricky.

My wonderful puppy grew into a mature dog with severe separation anxiety. This is a common psychological issue for Weims, but it can be heightened by the owner's lack of appropriate boundaries. As a pastor, I worked on the weekends, when our dog trainer traveled with Holly to shows. Without my presence, Holly was emotionally distressed, and she couldn't focus well enough to compete. The dog show world was no place for her.

Even though Holly didn't make a great show dog, she made up for it as a pet. We were inseparable. I've never found a dog that loved to snuggle as much as she. Wherever I went, Holly went with me. She became an extra pillow, a living thermal blanket in cold weather, and a friend. Jokingly, I would tell my wife that no one loved me more than Holly. But I know for Holly that sentiment was absolutely true. She was the perfect dog for me, and my life was better because she was in it.

In July of 2005, my wife and I were expecting our first child. For months we'd prepared our lives and home for her arrival. We painted and decorated the nursery. My wife and mother-in-law stitched together the perfect quilt for our upcoming blessing.

But a couple days before my daughter's due date, my wife went in to the doctor for a routine pre-delivery checkup. Her doctor couldn't find a heartbeat. In a panic my wife called me as they rushed her to the hospital.

My heart sank.

In all of our prenatal doctor visits and Lamaze classes, no one ever prepared us for this scenario. I joined my wife at the hospital only to discover that our baby had passed away. On my daughter's due date, the doctor induced my wife, and she delivered our stillborn baby girl.

It was the worst moment of my life.

During the hospital stay, I went home for a while to be alone. I wanted nothing more than to throw out all of the nursery furniture. I was so mad at everything that I didn't want to look at any reminders of our loss. I boiled inside as I tried to rationalize, understand, process, and cope with my daughter's death.

While at home, I let Holly out to run and relieve herself. She raced through the yard, her big ears flopping with each step. She didn't know how badly I hurt inside. She couldn't comprehend my sadness.

But she wanted to be with me.

As fast as she could, Holly finished her business and joined me inside the house on the chaise lounge chair. With the force of a joyous hurricane, she blasted into my arms. Her bobbed tail flitted from side to side faster than windshield wipers turned on high. She furiously licked at my face. And just like when she was a puppy, she crawled into my lap.

I snaked my arms around her heaving chest and pulled in close. Even though I'd lost my daughter, I still had Holly. Sure, a dog could never replace my own child, but when the world seemed to crumble around me, I was glad to have her. The pair of us sat on the chair together for a long while. My tears melted into her soft fur as I rubbed my face against her warm body. After a while, I regained my composure and headed back to join my wife.

The months following my daughter's stillbirth were filled with many moments of grief and sorrow, but Holly was almost always there to help me through them.

She was a godsend.

In my life's darkest valley, God used a Weimaraner to rescue me from my heartache and anguish and to allow me to heal over time.

Not a day goes by when I don't miss my daughter, Peace A. Young. But grief was always easier to manage when Miss Holly Berry curled up around my feet, nudged me out of bed, or cuddled up on my lap while I drove.

Survival of the Fittest

Catherine Ulrich Brakefield

When I was a child, my dad loved hunting and wanted to breed his own bird dogs. My mom always went along with what my dad wanted, so Dad bought a springer spaniel named Tango. She was a fantastic bird dog and beautiful in action running across the fields. She would spring up, peeking over the tall snapdragons and brush, her curly white ears always popping up a half inch higher than her head.

But before Dad could breed Tango to the winning pointer he'd signed up for, Tango became pregnant. And Tip was born.

I will never forget the day I first laid eyes on Tip. He was wet and wiggly, his eyes sealed shut. He inched his way toward mother's milk by smell and instinct.

Ten other puppies pushed him aside. Because he was the smallest, what some breeders would call the runt of the litter, he had a harder time fighting for the nipple. But did he fight! Every inch of the way to his mother's milk, sometimes to get pushed back, stepped over, even buried beneath the tiny bundles of fur battling for existence.

My siblings and I watched, amazed. Dad told us about the survival of the fittest. We kids were speechless. Did that mean Tip would die? Mom, our Christian example of compassion, let it be known to my survival-of-the-fittest father that this would not be the norm here. Mom made it my duty to make sure Tip got his fair share of Tango's milk. Maybe that was the reason for that special bond Tip had with us.

Many pups grew up looking like a smaller version of Tango, and Dad wanted to keep the largest and sell the rest. But he was outvoted by the rest of the family. We had formed a special attachment to the runt we named Tip because of the white tip on his tail that always waved like a flag when he was happy.

When I was eleven years old, I realized I was tall enough to reach up to our black saddlebred's neck, draw her head down, insert the bit, and place the leather bridle over her ears. I no longer needed Dad! Wow! Did I ever feel grown up. I tried to lift Dad's saddle and quickly realized it was much too heavy for me to swing up onto the mare. So I decided to ride her bareback. My next endeavor was to climb up on my mare's back.

I led the horse named Black Magic—Mage to my siblings and me—out of the stable. I got a wooden milk crate to stand on. Tip watched everything intently. By now he was nearly full grown, and I had taught him to heel on the leash, come when I called him, and, of course, stay when I wanted him to stay put.

Mage did a dance around my milk crate. I kept moving the crate, and she would step away, pushing her rear end outward. I needed help in the worst way. My knees were shaking by this time. I'd ridden her bareback twice before, but always under the supervision of my dad. How was I going to get up? I couldn't stop now. I'd be a quitter! Dad frowned on quitting and always told us not to give up.

I looked at Tip then back to Mage. "Tip, make Mage stay. Go on, you can do it!"

Tip's head moved from side to side.

"Come on, Tip. Keep her still." I was in trouble if Tip couldn't help me. "Tip, what kind of a man's best friend are you?" I pointed Tip to the spot, told him to sit, and then said firmly, "Stay."

I pulled Mage right in front of Tip and yanked downward on Mage's reins, then put the milk crate close to her side. Mage took a step forward. Then Tip stood, his legs spread apart as if to say, "Over my dead body." Mage stared down at this obstinate pup and pricked her ears forward, seemingly mesmerized by Tip's stare. That gave me just enough time to grab a handful of mane and jump up on her bare back.

I let out a sigh of relief and then looked at the kitchen window. Did Mom see me? Yep! She came out of the house, arms akimbo. "Did you get permission from your dad to ride Mage by yourself?"

That was definitely a question to avoid.

"Can I just ride her around the orchard? Don't worry, I'll be safe. Tip's going to come too."

Mom looked down at the multicolored pup. Tip looked back, wagged his tail, and yelped. "Well, okay. Tip, you be a good dog and keep her safe!"

That was to become Tip's top job throughout his years, keeping my siblings and me safe. Dad's words about survival of the fittest became our motto. With the ever-watchful Tip by our side, we had a fighting chance of surviving our childhood adventures.

One day Mage tripped while I was galloping down a lane. She fell to her knees, and I flew over her head and landed hard. With the wind knocked out of me, all I could do was lay there and gasp for air. Tip jumped in and licked my face. When I pointed to Mage's loose reins, Tip ran to her, grabbed her reins, and brought Mage back to me.

Needless to say, I was so afraid Mom and Dad wouldn't let me go riding alone again that I never told them about the incident. Tip never squealed on me!

179

I loved to read, and after reading *Tom Sawyer* and *Huckleberry Finn*, I decided to see what adventure I could find in the swampy area at the end of our road. I found a large stick, and Tip and I waded into the ankle-deep water. I even tried to hop onto a log and pretend it was a raft. But coming out of the swamp, we encountered three mean-looking dogs I had never seen before. They growled at me. The hair on their necks rose up like porcupine quills.

"Nice doggies," I said, thinking I could talk my way out of the situation. I tried to exude more confidence than I felt. Tip jumped in front of me, growling low, his teeth bared. Every time the dogs moved, he moved too, keeping his body between me and the dogs. I wished I had picked up a thicker and longer stick. Tip was no competition for these three dogs. Evidently the dogs thought so too. They began to circle us.

The dogs' eyes focused on Tip. I was so scared I couldn't scream, let alone run. Besides, I couldn't leave Tip. I couldn't run out on my buddy. I realized I hadn't told Mom where I'd gone. *Please*, I begged God, *I promise not to be disobedient again!* My vivid imagination depicted the scene of Tip's and my dead bodies lying in the swamp and Mom crying over me . . . something like what Huck went through.

But Tip had another idea. The dogs slowly moved in, stiff-legged. When they got three feet away from Tip, he hurtled his twenty-pound body at the largest dog, three times his size.

Tip grabbed him around the throat and gave it a twist, the same way I'd seen him do to a ground hog. The dog was knocked off his feet and lay still. Tip had blood on his teeth and mouth. He threw himself at the other large dog. The third hesitated, then Tip and he met on their haunches. Tip was dwarfed next to that animal's size.

I raised my stick, but before I could use it, the dog yelped and limped away. The other dog got up from the ground, growling low, and backed away. Tip was still outraged and practically flew after the third dog until my whistle called him back.

Tip immediately turned, ran to my side, and sniffed me, as if to make sure I was all right. His mouth was bloody. Parts of his white coat around his chest were stained scarlet. I wiped away most of it. I fought back my tears and reached into the swampy water to dab a wound on his neck and leg before heading home. "Tip, how am I going to tell Mom?"

By the time we got home, I had dreamed up a happy ending to my Huckleberry excursion. After all, Tom Sawyer was one great motivator for fabricating stories!

But it turned out I didn't need Tom Sawyer's made-up stories to get me out of trouble. The truth was all Mom wanted and needed. She proved to be my staunch supporter. Mom was a winner through and through.

Tip was the hero of the day, and when the man who owned the three dogs came by the house, he got an earful from my outraged mom while I watched from behind a curtain. Of course, hard as I tried to, I couldn't hear any of the conversation.

Mom was pregnant with her sixth child then. Watching that man back away from my mom was something to see. Tip sat in the doorway in full view before the glass storm door. The man pointed a finger at him, and Tip rose, legs spread. I believe he would have gone right through that window if the man had laid a hand on my mom. The man finally walked away. That was the end of the conversation.

And that's when Tip became the official guardian of us children. When we went bike riding, Mom would say, "Take Tip." When we were in our aboveground pool in the backyard, Tip was our lifeguard. He'd bark when we started to play too rough. Mom would stick her head out the door and say, "If you kids don't stop that, you'll have to get out of the pool."

Tip was the best hunting dog Dad ever had. "Look at that!" Dad would say as he showed us a bird he shot. "Tip didn't even disturb a feather bringing it back to me through that underbrush!" But Tip's true value was how he protected his family, that flag of a tail waving until the day he died.

I always had a Tip after that—or a Tippy, or Tippie so that our vet could tell them apart. But all those dogs bore the name Tip upon their small shoulders. My children would ask, "Mom, why do you always name one of our dogs Tip?"

That's when I'd say, "Because I'm hoping this puppy might live up to his namesake and be just half the dog my first Tip was."

Some of them came pretty close. I've witnessed more litters through the passing years, those tiny bundles of fur battling for existence against innumerable odds, like that first Tip. Yes, it's all about survival of the fittest. And with God's creatures by our side, we humans also have a fighting chance of surviving life's challenges.

Gotcha Day

Jen Reeder

I was standing in an animal shelter in New Mexico, palms sweating, as my dog tugged on the leash. Hardly anyone noticed—the place was a hive of activity. Volunteers peppered staff members with questions as others hurried past to take adoptable dogs for walks. Finally, I caught the eye of a "tween" girl, who approached me with another young lady. I thrust a bag of dog treats and supplies at them.

"Thanks!" she said. "Do you need a receipt?"

"No, but is there someone in charge whom I could speak with for a minute?" My voice shook.

They looked at me like I was nuts, then the younger one hollered, "Mom!" A harried but beautiful woman paused on her way to the office and changed course toward me.

That's when I started to cry. She gave me a wary look.

I wasn't going to return my dog—far from it. The day six years before when my husband, Bryan, and I adopted him was one of the happiest of my life (and I've been blessed with lots of happy days).

When we first met Rio, he was a dirty, emaciated twelve-week-old Labrador retriever mix sharing a cage with the rest of his unwanted littermates. It was clear he wasn't an alpha male—the other dogs were climbing all over him, and he had a bite mark on his cheek. But in the meet-and-greet room, his little tail never stopped wagging as he frolicked between Bryan and me. I felt an

A Dog of Dogs

If you've ever observed a working guide dog, you're not just looking at any ol' dog. That noble canine in a harness is a Dog of Dogs, worth more money than a shiny new Tesla car. Absolutely priceless to its visually impaired partner. And yet, when that leather harness comes off, it's quitting time. That working dog clocks out and turns into a lovable pet. Until the harness goes back on.

A working guide dog has been specially bred, raised, and trained to act as the eyes to guide a blind or visually impaired person. But here's what you don't see: dozens of loving hands—professionals and volunteers—who have carefully ushered that very dog from puppyhood to a working guide.

Back in 1942, Lois Merrihew and Don Donaldson had a dream: to provide service dogs to World War II veterans. They started with a German shepherd named Blondie who was rescued from the pound. Blondie was the first graduate of what eventually became Guide Dogs for the Blind, the largest guide dog school in the world.

To date, over 14,000 "teams"—defined as visually impaired human paired to a working guide—have graduated. The charity is entirely supported through private donations; not a penny is charged to the graduate. Anyone who is blind or visually impaired can apply for a dog, but there are some hoops to jump through. These dogs are trained to enhance a person's mobility and independence, to help them lead an active life.

urgent need to take him away from that place and give him the best life possible.

Since his "Gotcha Day," Rio has blossomed into an incredible companion. He's always up for a hike, a swim, a car ride, or a cuddle. He gets so excited when we meet other people or dogs that he wags his entire body. As one woman remarked, "He doesn't know a stranger, does he?"

An important task for puppy raisers, who foster pups from about eight weeks of age to sixteen to eighteen months, is socialization: exposing and preparing the puppy for buses, trains, and planes, for grocery stores and restaurants, for dentists and libraries and work settings. A guide dog will be expected to have impeccable manners and be comfortable in all situations.

"Recall" occurs when a puppy becomes a dog, ready for specialized training. The dog is returned to the GDB campus in San Rafael, California, or Boring, Oregon. For all kinds of reasons (cat or squirrel distraction, for one example), many dogs end up "career-changed" during training. Still wonderful, still well trained, but they're meant for a different destiny. Those dogs who continue toward becoming a guide will be custom matched to a partner for a two-week intensive program. Then comes graduation day, a four-hanky event, but the support from GDB doesn't end on that day. There is yearly follow-up and veterinary care; GDB is committed to helping a partnership thrive.

These dogs, they're something special. Labrador retrievers, golden retrievers, and Lab/golden crosses from GDB's own purebred stock, specially selected for excellent temperament, intelligence, and health.

The cuteness, though, comes naturally.

—Suzanne Woods Fisher

Because Rio is so friendly, I had him certified as a therapy dog so that we can visit hospital patients together. Dog lovers light up like a Christmas tree when they see him—it's amazing to watch him bring smiles to sick or stressed people. One of my favorite visits was with a little girl who hadn't learned to talk yet. But she and Rio communicated fluently: he kissed her cheeks, then she giggled and held out her doll for him to kiss. When he did, she couldn't contain her peals of laughter. I felt so proud of my boy.

Another time a patient in her forties was lying in bed and stroking Rio's ears when her husband and a doctor arrived. Because of client confidentiality, the doctor politely asked us to leave while they discussed the diagnosis. About five minutes later, Rio and I were strolling down the hallway with another therapy dog handler and her Chihuahua when we heard footsteps running behind us. We turned to find the doctor headed our way. A little winded from her sprint, the doctor said, "She could really use a visit from the dogs right now."

We didn't know the diagnosis, only that it must be bad.

When we reentered the room, I chirped, "Hello again!"

The husband smiled with sad eyes. The woman looked dazed. "I have stage 4 cancer," she said. "It came out of the blue."

We spent quite a while in that room. Usually Rio will lie down on the floor for a snooze during lengthy visits, but he kept sitting up and staring at the woman. It was like he knew something heavy was going on and wanted her to be able to see him. His instincts were good; she looked at him frequently. When we said our good-byes, she gave me a teary look and said, "Thank you so much for coming."

Rio has brought comfort not only to countless strangers but to our little family. Five days before the second anniversary of Rio's Gotcha Day, I donated a kidney to my husband. We'd traveled to a transplant center six hours away from home and needed to stay nearby for a month in case Bryan's body rejected my kidney. Our pup adapted to life in a hotel, spending plenty of time curled up between us on the couch but also reminding us when it was time to take a walk outside—we needed to exercise even though it was painful to stand. Rio helped us relax during that stressful time and made our recovery infinitely more enjoyable. Everything went so well that we were sent home a week early.

So as I stood in front of the woman from the shelter on the sixth anniversary of Rio's Gotcha Day, I wanted to tell her how important it was that her organization had brought us together. The odds had been stacked against Rio—the shelter had been overcrowded and had to euthanize an average of nineteen dogs and cats a day—a day!—for space. Our adoption packet had included a letter from a local veterinarian thanking us for saving an animal from certain death. How many pets with Rio's potential had been put down simply because there wasn't enough room for them?

But the community knew the euthanasia rate was abhorrent and raised millions of dollars to build a state-of-the-art adoption facility—the one in which I was now standing. I was overwhelmed by gratitude for their efforts to save the lives of so many animals. I wanted shelter employees and volunteers to know their work mattered. Someone needed to see Rio, to understand how he'd affected my life as well as the lives of others.

It's a lot of pressure for a minute-long conversation.

The shelter manager smiled at me, and I dove in.

"This is Rio . . . he's a therapy dog . . . I love him so much . . . I'm sorry to be so emotional . . ."

She knelt to pet Rio, and he tried to lick her ears while wagging with his usual gusto. I pulled a Maxwell Medallion from the Dog Writers Association of America out of my pocket. It was engraved with my name and "Best Magazine Article: Rescue." I offered it to the shelter manager.

"Rio's changed my life," I choked out as her daughter listened, eyes wide. "I want you to have this medal to know what an impact it made to save his life. Your work is so important—thank you for all you do for animals and the people who love them."

The manager's eyes were moist with tears as I made a hasty exit. Rio padded along next to me, ready for our next move, tail waving like a flag.

On the drive home, I took the liberty of letting my tears flow freely. Rio licked them from my cheeks before settling into a nap. But as we passed the "Welcome to Colorful Colorado" sign and reentered our home state, he rested his chin on my arm. I grinned, knowing my sweet boy was exactly where he was meant to be and feeling full of anticipation for what the next six years might bring.

Strays in the Snow

Lonnie Hull DuPont

My older sister Peg is a wonderful and generous human being. Anyone who knows her knows this. I've been the recipient of her kindness more times than I can count. Of course, as my older sister, she can still on occasion be a little bossy toward me and treat me like . . . well . . . a kid sister—even though we're both adults. But that's okay. I learned early on that my good sister Peg is, as they say, all bark and no bite.

A few years ago, my husband and I bought a farmhouse in Michigan from Peg and her husband. It included an acre of land but did not include any of the farm buildings. A few miles away, Peg and her husband had a cattle ranch, and they had some plans for the barn behind our farmhouse.

One winter there was a heavy snowstorm that stopped midday, and my brother-in-law graciously plowed out our driveway. Shortly thereafter, local news stations warned that a second storm was right behind this one and that listeners had a three-hour window to get groceries, gas up, pick up kids, or do whatever else needed to be done. Off I went to the store.

An hour later I arrived home with a trunk full of groceries. The farmhouse sat on a plain surrounded by fields, but the road was a fairly busy truck route. My husband and I had gotten in the habit of pulling into the driveway, turning around at the barn, and then parking next to the house, nose out. This way we didn't back onto the road with semi-trucks barreling by.

On this day, I did my usual turnaround, parked near the back door, hopped out of the car, and popped the trunk. I grabbed a couple of bags, and when I turned toward the house, I saw the most surprising thing.

Standing in the snow next to the driveway were two large and gorgeous husky dogs. They appeared out of nowhere. I hadn't seen them until that very moment, and they were like some kind of wintry vision appearing before me in the glassy snow. I stopped in my tracks.

The dogs were squarely in my path to the house. Fortunately, when I spoke to them, they wagged their snowy tails. I placed a grocery bag between the dogs and me and slowly moved past them to the back door. They followed.

I figured I should feed them. We didn't have a dog or dog food, so I piled two bowls with canned chicken and took them outside. The dogs were still there, as if they were waiting, and I fed them on the stoop. One was clearly alpha and stepped in front of the other, who waited respectfully, even though there were two bowls. They were handsome dogs—one had two different colored eyes—and they were very polite. Both dogs had collars, but only one had a tag. The dog let me check it, but the names had worn off.

Now what? I thought. I knew I did not want them running into the road. Animals never lasted on this road with the truck traffic; we had seen this too many times.

At that time, the barn was not occupied. I had a key, so I picked the food bowls up, and the dogs followed me. I led them into the barn, put the food down, and left them inside. At least the dogs would be safe from traffic and from the oncoming snowstorm.

I called my sister. Peg answered, sounding unusually harried.

"Hey," I said. "There were two stray huskies in my yard, so I'm just letting you know I've put them in the barn until I figure out whose they are."

"Oh, that's just great," Peg huffed. "Now they'll make a mess all over the barn."

I paused, a little surprised. "Well, it *is* a barn," I said, "not a house, and I'll be sure to clean up after them. But I don't want them to get killed on the road."

"Okay," Peg said. "Go ahead. But I really need to go now." And we said our good-byes.

I called the local police, assuring them this was not an emergency. I told them where I lived and that I had no idea what to do about these beautiful dogs.

"I think we're in luck," the officer said. "A few miles down your road, there's a woman who breeds huskies. They probably came from her. I'll get her number for you."

Excellent. I called the woman, whose name was Caroline. She answered the phone, and I told her I thought that two of her dogs had strayed to my house.

"No," she said, "they aren't mine. All my dogs are accounted for. But I'd be glad to come over and see if I know whose they are."

Caroline showed up shortly, and we headed for the barn. The dogs were friendly still, though they seemed a little puzzled as to why they were locked up. Caroline petted them and looked them over, handling them with ease. "I don't recognize them," she said, "but lots of farmers out here have huskies."

I didn't realize that.

"I think you should call the local radio station. They make announcements about lost dogs."

I smiled inside. When my husband and I first moved there, we'd laughed at the local radio station when we heard them announce the local bowling scores. But this suggestion made sense.

And it worked. The next day a young woman with a raspy voice called my house, sobbing. "I think you have my dogs . . ." For some reason, her two dogs had gone running from home two days ago, and the owner's voice was literally hoarse from calling them.

I called Caroline, who offered to come to the house for the reunion. "You'll want to know they're really hers," she advised. "Full breed dogs are very popular with companies that do testing."

Another thing I didn't realize.

Caroline showed up, then the owner. Before we relinquished the dogs, Caroline questioned the young woman. "Please don't be offended," said Caroline, "but we want to make certain your dogs have found their true owner, okay?"

The woman understood, and once she passed muster, we headed for the barn. Then there could be no doubt these were her fur babies. They licked her face and whined while she cried and rubbed their thick fur.

All ended well.

So I called Peg to report that the dogs were gone and there was no mess in the barn. That's when I learned that, the day before, at the very time I was telling Peg about the dogs, at the very time she complained that they would make a mess in the barn, she was taking care of an ailing calf.

In her house.

Upstairs.

In her bathtub.

All bark. No bite.

The Sound of Home

Susan C. Willett

The barking was loud and intense as I approached the backyard of a home in a nearby neighborhood. I could hear drumming paws running and skittering across the deck, and as I approached, the barks and howls and cries crescendoed into a near frenzy. I could pick out one particularly loud and piercing woof; it was a huge sound, as if it came from a Doberman or rottweiler.

Suddenly a shiny black nose sprouted between the unpainted slats of the deck. Another nose pushed its way above the first. There was a pause in the sound barrage as the noses drew in my scent in audible snorts.

I heard the sound of a door opening, and a woman I assumed was Cindy directed me to the stairs, at the top of which was a gate through which I could see two puppies.

I recognized the smaller of the two pups from the photos on Petfinder.com; within her glossy black fur, two bright eyes offered a glint of playful intelligence that foretold mischief beyond the garden-variety puppy shenanigans. Her tail drew large circles—no mere back and forth for this girl—as she danced her way across the deck. She was the one I had come here to meet.

The other pup—a houndish-looking creature—either had one too many legs or they were too long or maybe he was still trying to figure out how they worked; he tripped and stumbled but never quite fell as he bounded over to me. He leapt over the smaller dog, knocked into a table, looked up at me with a joyful and goofy expression, and squeaked out a princess bark.

Then the little black puppy opened her mouth and barked like a rottie.

Wait. What? I thought. *Big dog equals big bark. Small dog equals small bark.*

"I know you only came to see Black Beauty." Cindy motioned to the puppy in question. "But she came with Spike here, and he's the only one left of his litter. I thought you might want to meet him too."

Spike? Mr. Princess Bark is named Spike? Spike wagged his tail so hard I thought he'd sprain his wagger and galumphed across the deck. Beauty stayed close by his side, matching him bounce for bounce.

As Cindy opened the gate to allow me up on the deck, I decided I would have to change Black Beauty's name. Her namesake was a horse, and it just wouldn't do. And Spike? He was no more a Spike than I was Ernest Hemingway.

Cindy told me what she knew of the puppies, how they had been pulled from a kill shelter in Louisiana and brought here to New Jersey, where—due to expansive spay and neuter programs in our state—there are fewer adoptable puppies and therefore more demand.

She suggested I sit on the paw-print-covered wicker couch, and the two puppies immediately scrambled over to me, skidding into my legs as if neither of them had adequate brakes. Beauty jumped up next to me and licked my ear. I leaned in to her and inhaled her puppiness—a smell of warmth and sweetness that comes in as a close second to the scent of babies, for those who, like me, admit to sniffing both baby heads and puppy breath.

Spike—I really needed to change his name—rolled over on the deck, his long legs waving in the air like a flipped beetle. His tail swept back and forth and his eyes looked up at me with a clear belly rub request.

I imagined these two cowering in some dark holding pen, their futures only made possible by unknown kindhearted souls who removed them from a terrible fate and brought them to this place, this time, and me. I had come here to see Black Beauty, but how could I take her home and leave Spike?

Besides, as much as I didn't want to think about it, I had room for two dogs in my life, or I would soon.

My four-year-old terrier, Rosie, had died only two weeks ago, from an aggressive form of liver cancer. A scruffy Frisbee-catching, squirrel-chasing, ball-obsessed pup, she loved squeaky toys and hated cats—and lived her life at full speed.

My other dog, Pasha—a Keeshond mix—was an elderly thirteen, hanging on with the help of several medications to control his kidney issues, heart problems, and arthritis. He needed help standing up, tottered a bit when he walked, and sometimes got stuck in corners, forgetting how to back up and get out.

Yes, he was old, our Pasha. But he still loved performing his perimeter check each time we took him outside, ambling slowly around our yard, nose to the ground next to our fence. As he investigated evidence of intruders who breached our borders—squirrels and rabbits and chipmunks—his fluffy tail swept like a happy flag over his back.

I knew Pasha was going to die. I expected it. I hated it, was distressed at the thought of it, and avoided talking about it, but Pasha had lived a long and happy life since we adopted him.

I could see the end coming toward us like a slow-moving summer shower—the kind you cannot quite outwalk. But it was inevitable, and I had been preparing myself and my family emotionally for months.

But not Rosie. Not four-year-old Rosie.

No, I couldn't accept the destructive storm that had enveloped her. One day she was leaping in a graceful arc to pluck a Frisbee from the air. The next day I was on the phone with the vet, my hand shaking with denial as I tried to write down the strange harsh letters that spelled cancer.

I railed at her disease. It infuriated me. It wasn't fair. To her. To me. To my family.

She died at home, the whole family gathered around her. We had only six weeks from her diagnosis to her death. She passed easily, her last breath a soft sigh, gone with a whisper.

After Rosie's death, I tipped into darkness, sobbing at the sight of one of Rosie's squeaky balls, collapsing into a puddle when I reached for one leash instead of two. My brain was cottony and tangled, thick with grief.

It was in that state that I realized I had to face the unthinkable: that Pasha would join Rosie soon, and I might be left in a home without dogs. Losing one dog was excruciating. Losing two would be unbearable. A home without a dog is a body without a soul.

I needed to adopt another dog. Not a replacement. Never. But I did not want to even imagine the possibility of coming home and finding the house dark and quiet, with silence replacing the *thunk thunk* of tails wagging against the clothes dryer.

I knew that making a decision when grief ruled my every hour was not the best plan, so I sought input from my husband and teenaged son, as well as my daughter, who had just started her freshman year at film school.

While everyone agreed it was too soon to think about another dog in the family, none of us felt we could face a dogless home. Thus, merely a week after we lost Rosie, I sat in front of my laptop, and with clumsy, heavy fingers opened up Petfinder.com. Feeling disloyal, tears splashing on my keyboard, I apologized to my sweet terrier and entered my zip code.

I clicked through dozens of photos. Objectively they were adorable, but my *aww* reflex was broken.

I knew I wasn't looking for another Rosie. But every one of those puppies was *not* Rosie. And like a stubborn child who wants only what she can't have, my heart was throwing a tantrum; I wanted my dog back.

I showed some of the entries to my husband. This one? That one? He was hurting too, but he was able to look at the pictures and feel something. "How about her?" he asked when I clicked on a photo of a small black puppy with a sweet face and a charming smile.

Which was why I was here, sitting on rickety outdoor furniture on the deck of someone I barely knew, having my face cleaned by two exuberant puppies.

I watched as the houndy puppy matched the black dog's zigs and zags, gamboling along with her. It was easy to see he idolized her, so eager was he to play with her, to emulate her, to stay by her side.

Even if they weren't bound by blood, these two had a connection borne from their shared history. The concept of separating them, of being responsible for another's loss, was unthinkable. Though I had not imagined being a three-dog family, it seemed right to adopt both of these puppies, to bring this pair into our home. We would love them with Pasha, as long as he continued to enjoy a decent quality of life. These two would have each other when the inevitable loss came.

The decision was made. I was going to adopt both Not Black Beauty and Not Spike.

I still had to get agreement from the rest of the family, but it wasn't hard. My heart wasn't the only one shattered by Rosie's passing.

Cindy brought our new family members to our house that Friday evening, when my daughter and her new boyfriend would be coming home for a visit. Over the past week, we had come up with more suitable names for the pair, agreeing on Lilah for the black puppy—the word means "night" in Hebrew—and Jasper for our goofy hound, in honor of a favorite humorous author, Jasper Fforde.

I barely heard Cindy's instructions as she handed me two bright red folders and two leashes, dogs still attached. She gave a tearful hug to each of her charges—and to me—and left quickly, while I marveled at the emotional strength required to care for and then give up these beautiful souls—even to a good home.

Pasha struggled up on wobbly legs, trying to see through his clouded eyes. I sat next to him, concerned that the energetic youngsters would knock over our unsteady elder statesman. Instead, both puppies approached him gently, perhaps sensing his infirmities.

Noses touched. Tails wagged softly. Pasha approved.

Early Monday morning, barely forty-eight hours after Jasper and Lilah arrived, and a little less than three weeks after Rosie died, Pasha took a turn for the worse. He couldn't pull himself up into a standing position, and wobbled so much once we helped him there that he was unable to walk. Worse, his breathing sounded more like panting, and even lying on the floor, he seemed agitated, unable to get comfortable. We sat up with him all night, staying by his side, surrounding him with love, and giving him the pets and snuggles and attention that he thrived on.

> "Until one has loved an animal, a part of one's soul remains unawakened."
>
> —Anatole France

I think Pasha hung on for those weeks while Rosie got sicker and after she died. Somehow, he knew— I'm sure he *knew*—that we simply could not be left alone. But once the puppies came into our home, our old man didn't have to work so hard. We had two dogs who could fill the huge empty space that Rosie left—and the one he would leave too.

In the morning, as a family, we made the sorrowful pilgrimage to the vet in that awful act of ultimate kindness, to ease Pasha's obvious suffering, and to let him go.

We drove home carrying the weight of an empty collar and hearts full of grief. As we walked through the garage, we could hear puppy whines of welcome from within our house. I opened the door to an orchestra of rottie and princess barks, joyous howls and moans, and the *thunk thunk* of tails against the dryer.

Once again, we were a double-dog home.

Acknowledgments

Many thanks to the hard-working, animal-loving people at Revell, a division of Baker Publishing Group, for keeping the vision going, and extra thanks to my extraordinary editor, Dr. Vicki Crumpton.

About the Contributors

Donna Acton is a licensed veterinary technician who has worked in veterinary hospitals for over three decades. As the daughter of a veterinarian, she has had a lifelong interest in helping pets and the people they live with, and her professional focus now is behavior training for dogs and cats.

Judy Auger resides in Tehachapi, California, a small but growing town in the mountains. She enjoys reading, writing, learning languages, and speaking them with friends or with travelers. In her other long-ago life, she taught college-level Spanish as well as secondary level English, Spanish, and French.

Sheryl Bass earned a bachelor's degree in psychology from Florida State University, a master's degree in social work from Colorado State University, and a master's degree in print journalism from the University of Colorado in Boulder. Sadly, Lyric passed away at the ripe old age of sixteen in July 2016. Sheryl now lives in a suburb outside of Chicago with her supportive husband, Neil, and their loving rescue dogs, Asher and Piper.

Lisa Begin-Kruysman (www.lisabegin-kruysmanauthor.com) has made man's best friend the focus of her award-winning works of fiction and nonfiction and social media platform since 2010. She is the torchbearer for the venerable National Dog Week Movement established in 1928 to make humans more responsible for the canines in their lives. She works and resides in Ocean County, New Jersey. Also see www.facebook.com/NatDogWeek/ and www.nationaldogweekbook.wordpress.com.

Catherine Ulrich Brakefield is an award-winning author of faith-based historical romances that include *Wilted Dandelions* and *Swept into Destiny*. The second of her four-book Destiny series, *Into Destiny's Whirlwind*, will debut soon. She lives in Michigan with her husband and their Arabian horses. You can visit her at CatherineUlrichBrakefield.com, Facebook.com/CatherineUlrich Brakefield, and HopesHeartsandHoofbeats.com.

Melody Carlson (www.melodycarlson.com) is one of the most prolific novelists of our time. With more than two hundred novels published and book sales topping seven million, she's received numerous national writing awards. She makes her home in central Oregon.

Tye Cranfill is the author of many books.

Dr. W. Alan Dixon, Sr., lives in Northern California with his best friend and wife, Xochitl. He has two adult sons, AJ and Xavier, a daughter-in-law, Mallory, and a doggie daughter, Jazzy. Fueled with a desire for learning, he continually works to develop secular and ministry organizational leadership programs, and his passion is to equip leaders with practical tools to help make them success-ful. You can reach Dr. Dixon via LinkedIn at www.linkedin.com /in/mralandixon or Twitter at @mralandixon.

Xochitl (so-cheel) E. Dixon serves as a writer for Our Daily Bread Ministries. She is currently working on a devotional for dog lovers who desire deeper relationships with God and others. She enjoys being a mom; traveling with her husband, Alan; photography; singing; and trying to convince her husband they need more dogs. She shares encouragement devotions and prayers on her blog at www.xedixon.com and through *Our Daily Bread* at www.odb .org/subscriptions.

Andrea Doering is an editor and the author of several children's books and short stories. She has been the lucky caretaker of six dogs thus far. She holds an MA in English/creative writing from the University of Maine and lives with her family in New York.

Chrissy Drew lives in Northern California with her darlin', Mike. She's been published in seven other anthologies and is currently editing her first book in a contemporary romance novella series. She would love to hear from you. You can find her at chrissydrew .com or facebook.com/AuthorChrissyDrew.

Lonnie Hull DuPont is an award-winning poet, book editor, and author of several nonfiction books. She frequently writes about animals, and her most recent book is a memoir of sorts, *Kit Kat & Lucy: The Country Cats Who Changed a City Girl's World*.

Wanda Dyson is the critically acclaimed author of nine "high octane" suspense novels and the coauthor with Tina Zahn of *Why I Jumped*. She is currently working on the autobiography of Hall of Fame pro wrestler Tully Blanchard. You can visit her website at www.WandaDyson.com.

Suzanne Woods Fisher is a bestselling, award-winning author who is a puppy raiser (ten and counting!) and breeder custodian for

Guide Dogs for the Blind (www.guidedogs.com). She likens raising puppies to eating potato chips—you can't stop at just one!

Denise Fleck was raised by a Great Dane and has spent her life loving animals. She has written scores of magazine articles, authored ten books, and is the proud recipient of two "Muse Awards" from the Cat Writers Association and three Maxwell Medallions from the Dog Writers Association, including "Best Children's Book." A former film studio publicist, Fleck followed her heart, leaving entertainment to work with animals, and developed her own pet first aid and CPCR curriculum, personally teaching more than 15,000 humans plus millions more via TV appearances. Learn more at www.PetSafetyCrusader.com.

Susy Flory (www.susyflory.com) is a *New York Times* bestselling writer. She directs the West Coast Christian Writers Conference near San Francisco. Her newest book is *The Sky Below* with Scott Parazynski, the only man ever to both fly in space and summit Mount Everest. She loves to help her daughter, Teddy, who works in wildlife rehabilitation and has a blind owl who lives in the kitchen.

When she's not teaching middle school history or hanging out at the barn with her Thoroughbred ex-racehorse Knight, **Susan Friedland-Smith** cuddles her black Doberman, Missie, and tosses the tennis ball into the pool for Tigger, the golden retriever. Susan's award-winning blog, *Saddle Seeks Horse*, celebrates the horse- and hound-centric lifestyle of the everyday equestrian—the grown-up horse girl with alfalfa in her purse and dog hair on her dashboard. Follow Susan and hubby Mark's adventures on her blog saddleseekshorse.com, Instagram @SaddleSeeksHorse, or Facebook's *Saddle Seeks Horse* fan page.

Sherri Gallagher (www.sherrigallagher.com) has been participating in K9 search and rescue since 1998. Her books can be found on Amazon and are based on her own dogs or SAR team member canines. Her teen trilogy, Growing Up SAR, includes the novels *Turn*, *Go Find*, and *Bark Alert*, and her novel *Sophie's Search* releases soon as the first book in her new romance series, Searching the North Country. Her Facebook page is SherriGallagherAuthor, and the team Facebook page is GSSARDA.

Michelle Janene is a teacher and an indie author of Christian fantasy. She has released the Changed Heart Series, been included in many anthologies, and was featured in *Guideposts* magazine. Michelle founded Strong Tower Press to assist other writers. You can connect with her on Facebook at Michelle Janene-Turret Writing or Strong Tower Press, Twitter @MichelleJaneneM, or read her blogs at StrongTowerPress.com.

Marci Kladnik, her rescue dog, and four rescue cats live in a small California town with no stoplights or mail delivery. A retired graphic designer and medical technical writer, she turned her talents to championing feral cats in 2007. Involved in TNR and feral rescue, she sat on the board of directors of Catalyst for Cats from 2007 to 2013 and in her spare time still traps and fosters local feral cats and kittens. Her award-winning bi-weekly cat column ran for seven years in three newspapers and on the www.catalystforcats.org website; she is an award-winning photographer and winner of the 2015 Kari Winters Rescue and Rehabilitation Award for her writings on www.catster.com; and she is currently president of the Cat Writers' Association.

Audrey Leach loves dogs, especially rusty-colored ones. She also loves books and people, so she is fortunate to work for a wonderful publishing house with wonderful coworkers. When she's not working, you'll usually find her in her flower garden—curled up with a book, of course!

Dana Mentink is a two-time American Christian Fiction Writers Carol Award winner plus a Romantic Times Reviewer's Choice Award and a Holt Medallion winner. She is a national bestselling author of over thirty-five titles in the suspense and lighthearted romance genres, including a dog-themed fiction series for Harvest House Publishers. She loves to be home with her husband, "Papa Bear" Mike, daughters Yogi and Boo Boo, a nutty terrier, a chubby box turtle, and a feisty parakeet. Visit her at danamentink.com or find her on Instagram @dana_mentink and on Facebook.

Sandra Murphy lives in the shadow of the Arch in St. Louis, Missouri. She writes about dogs, wildlife, and eco-friendly topics as well as short and long fiction. Her collection of short stories, *From Hay to Eternity: Ten Tales of Crime and Deception*, warns, "It's always the quiet ones you have to worry about." Look for her articles in *Animal Wellness*, *Sniff and Barkens*, and *Natural Awakenings* magazines.

Sarah Parshall Perry is the author of *Sand in My Sandwich (and Other Motherhood Messes I'm Learning to Love)* and *Mommy Needs a Raise (Because Quitting's Not an Option)*, and the coauthor of *When the Fairy Dust Settles*. Her stories, essays, and op-eds have been published in *The Federalist*, *Town Hall*, *The Daily Caller*, *Baltimore City Paper*, and *Christianity Today*, among others. Sarah received her JD from the University of Virginia School of Law and currently works as Partnership Director for the Family Research Council in Washington, DC. She has two cats, two dogs, three kids, and one old farm home, into which her husband thinks he's going to fit another dog.

Dusty Rainbolt is the author of the award-winning books *Cat Scene Investigator: Solve Your Cat's Litter Box Mystery*, *Kittens for Dummies*, *Ghost Cats*, and *Cat Wrangling Made Easy:*

Maintaining Peace & Sanity in Your Multicat Home. She also penned the historical mystery *Death Under the Crescent Moon* and sci-fi comedy *All the Marbles*, and coauthored the outrageous Four Redheads of the Apocalypse fantasy series. She's past president of the Cat Writers' Association and three-time recipient of the Friskies Writer of the Year Award. Check out her websites DustyCatWriter.com and StupidGravityPress.com.

Jen Reeder is an award-winning freelance journalist and president of the Dog Writers Association of America. Her work has appeared in *Family Circle, The Christian Science Monitor, The Dallas Morning News, Modern Dog, Modern Cat,* The American Animal Hospital Association's *Trends Magazine, Tails Pet Magazine, AKC Family Dog, The Huffington Post, Shape,* and many other publications. She volunteers as a therapy dog handler with her Labrador retriever mix, Rio, and she founded the nonprofit Rock 1 Kidney after donating her left kidney to her husband in 2012. Visit her online at jenreeder.com or rock1kidney.org.

A communicator by nature and a writer with heart, **Maggie Sabatier-Smith,** speaker, life coach, author, is a catalyst for change. Founder/president of Called To Action (www.CalledToAction.com), Sabatier-Smith, who is known as Coach Maggie, is a sought-after blogger because of her smart wit and reader retention. She is also a columnist for *Chispa!* magazine (www.chispamagazine.com) and communicates the message of purpose in her personal blog (www.CalledToAction.com/blog).

Kathrine Smith discovered her lifelong passion for animals at a very early age. She grew up in Texas in a remote, untamed area where nature and the wilderness nurtured her. She has worked extensively with zoological parks in reproductive physiology and conservation of endangered species, in addition to pursuing her strong interest in animal behavior and strengthening the human-animal bond. Kathrine cares for and manages numerous feral cat colonies and is deeply committed to animal rescue, as well as inspiring positive changes.

Lauraine Snelling is the award-winning author of over seventy novels, including the beloved Red River of the North series. When not writing, she can be found paintbrush in hand, creating flowers and landscapes. She and her husband, Wayne, live in the Tehachapi Mountains in California.

Leanne Southall resides in Pasadena, California, with her husband, Scott, and daughter Morgan. Their full house includes Marty, foster dog Buddy, kitten Chloe, and cat Rory. Their favorite part of the day is when the whole family snuggles onto the bed together, whiskers and paws aplenty! Marty is currently employed as CEO—Canine Executive Officer—of The Long Leash; you can say hello on Instagram @thelongleash or www.thelongleashlocal.com.

Claudia Wolfe St. Clair is an artist, writer, art therapist, and *anam cara* from Toledo, Ohio. You can read more from her in the Callie Smith Grant collection *The Horse of My Heart*.

After more than ten years of pursuing her dream of publication, **Missy Tippens**, a pastor's wife and mom of three from near Atlanta, Georgia, made her first sale to Harlequin Love Inspired in 2007. Her books have since been nominated for the Booksellers' Best, Holt Medallion, ACFW Carol Award, Gayle Wilson Award of Excellence, Maggie Award, Beacon Contest, RT Reviewer's Choice Award, and the Romance Writers of America RITA® Award. Visit Missy at www.missytippens.com, twitter.com/MissyTippens, and facebook.com/missy.tippens.readers.

A citizen of both the United States and Canada, **Delores E. Topliff** loves scenery and landscapes anywhere, plus family, grandchildren, friends, college teaching, mission trips, travel, and her homes in Minnesota and in Mississippi. She enjoys wildlife, gives convincing moose calls, and makes jewelry from just about anything, including porcupine quills. She has four published children's books plus historical novels now offered by the Seymour Literary Agency. Follow her at Delores Topliff on Facebook and delorestopliff.com, and her blog at mbtponderers.blogspot.com.

Susan C. Willett is a writer, humorist, and blogger whose award-winning original stories, poems, and humor appear in print and online, including her website LifeWithDogsAndCats.com and on Facebook, Twitter, and Instagram. She shares her home with dogs Lilah, Jasper, and Tucker, as well as cats Dawn, Athena, Elsa Clair, and Calvin T. Katz, The Most Interesting Cat in the World™, whose photo went viral and who now has his own social media accounts. Look for Susan's soon-to-be-published novel #*Wheres AzaleaBear* and an as-yet-untitled memoir that captures the joy, wonder, and laughter of life in a multispecies household. Susan has plenty of inspiration for her work, often finding it hiding in a box, splashing through a mud puddle, or taking up an entire couch.

Cyle Young is thankful God blessed him with the uniqueness of being an ADD-riddled . . . *SQUIRREL!* . . . binge writer. Not unlike the classic video game Frogger, Cyle darts back and forth between various writing genres. He crafts princess picture books, devotionals for fathers, and epic fantasy tales. Learn more about Cyle on his website www.cyleyoung.com.

About the Compiler

Callie Smith Grant loves animals of all kinds. She is the author of many animal stories, the author of several books for young readers, and the compiler of the anthologies *The Dog Next Door*, *The Cat in the Window*, *The Dog at My Feet*, *The Cat in My Lap*, and *The Horse of My Heart*.

Few creatures are as noble and soul-stirring as the horse. They give us a taste of wildness and yet make us feel at home.

This beautiful collection of stories will inspire and move us in the same way these marvelous beasts capture our hearts and imagination.

Enjoy These Uplifting Tales
of the Cats **We Love**

In this charming collection of true stories, you will find cats of all shapes, sizes, and demeanors. Each of them has played an important part in the lives of their humans. So grab a cup of coffee, find a comfortable chair, curl up with the special cat in your life, and enjoy these uplifting tales.

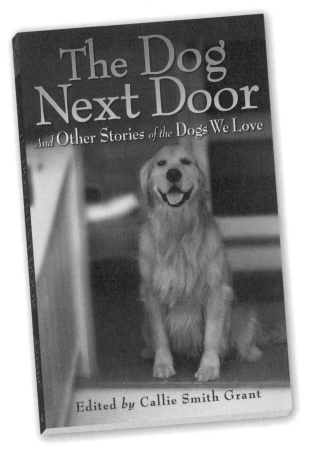

A PLAYFUL bat of a string. A BORED yawn. A TENDER purr at the touch of your hand.

The Cat in the Window is a delightful collection of true stories that celebrate the cats in our lives.